THE CAMPER VAN BIBLE

GLOVEBOX EDITION

The essential compact reference for the road, with extra checklists

MARTIN DOREY

CONWAY

LONDON · OXFORD · NEW YORK · NEW DELHI · SYDNEY

Contents

INTRODUCTION

Hello! Thanks for picking up this book. I hope it will become
a really useful addition to your camper van or motorhome, whether you
own one now or in the future. If you dream of buying one but haven't
quite got there yet, then please let this book help you to make it happen.
It will.

I call this *The Glovebox Edition* of *The Camper Van Bible* because I want
it to be a book that's really useful, both at home and when you are away.
I want it to be a constant and useful companion that you can refer to as
and when you need it. All the information inside has been written to be
useful in some way or another, either before you go or when you are on
the road, and I sincerely hope it is.

But, after you've used this book for a while and have got into the
rhythm of life on the road, I hope you'll pass it on – along with everything
you've learned from your own travels – to someone else. Don't let it fester
on a bookshelf or get lost in a rarely cleaned corner of the van. It's meant
to be used, abused, scribbled in and passed on. That's the point.

Every little bit of know-how or experience that's in this book comes
from a lifetime (well, more than 30 years) of sleeping in cars, vans
and motorhomes, travelling around the UK and Europe and spending
weeks on end on the road. It also comes from talking to people, making
friends, listening to manufacturers and campers and poking about in
hundreds of campers and motorhomes as a judge on the Motorhome
Design Award for the Caravan and Motorhome Club. I hope that you'll
be able to add your own experiences to it and make this copy – the one
you have in your hand right now – the most useful one yet. For that
reason we've left a few pages blank at the end. It sounds a bit of a cliché
to say that I want you to write your own story. But I do.

Camper vans and motorhomes have given me so many great
experiences over the years, from waking up to six inches of snow to
cooking for a crowd, and I have gained something from every moment.

I hope this book helps you to get some for yourself too. Of course, not all memories are brilliant, but that is all part of the pact you sign when you turn the key for the first time.

Camper van and motorhome ownership is a journey in itself. There are bumps in the road, hairpins, long easy straights and dead ends. This book, if I have done it right, will help you to navigate all of them with a smile on your face.

OK? Let's hit the road.

What's inside

The Camper Van Bible, first published in 2016, set out to be the be-all and end-all of camper van ownership. I wanted it to inspire anyone and everyone to dream of starry nights in the wild and get the most out of their van or dreams of owning a van.

This book, as I have said already, is about living with a van and making the most of it. Which is why it's full of advice, tips, lists and stuff that you might need help with. I'd still like it to give you itchy feet or wanderlust, but I also want it to help you do it successfully. And for that reason it's as practical as it can be. But hopefully never boring.

The first section, 'Before you go', is for anyone who wants to read about finding the perfect van, setting it up for travelling, preparing lists for going away and booking campsites. It's also got a load of information on types of places to stay, useful books to take and even prioritising packing.

The second part of the book is for the time you spend 'on the road'. This is stuff you might find useful when you are away. This includes information on clean air schemes, avoiding bad backs, finding campsites and how not to make a mess of servicing your motorhome.

It's all useful stuff and is why we've called this *The Glovebox Edition*. Because, we hope, that is where it belongs – right where you need it, for when you need it most.

Part One

DREAMS DO COME TRUE

It's really happening, isn't it?

Yes it is.

We're getting a camper van.

Yes we are.

Whooooppppeeee!!!!

You know that feeling? I do. Many others do too. It's a dream about to come true. Buying a camper van is such an exciting time. And gosh there are so many choices. So many options. So much to decide.

So I've tried to make it as simple as I can for you.

No book on camper vans and motorhomes would be complete without a buying guide. It's one of the biggest commitments you can make and, I hope, one of the best decisions you'll ever make, too. Get it right and you'll be drifting off into the sunset. Get it wrong and you could land yourself a headache.

But you won't will you?

No.

Whooooppppeeee!!!!

BUYING A CAMPER VAN

You have your heart set on a camper van or motorhome?
Fantastic. I look forward to meeting up with you on the road. But first, before you buy, there are a lot of questions you need to ask yourself.

I have listed them in detail in the following pages so that you'll know what to look for and what kind of recommendations can be made.

Big decision coming up, right? Buying a 'leisure vehicle' is a big commitment, both in time and money. Will you get to use it often enough? Will it keep its value? Will you be able to drive it every day?

Before you commit, there are some important decisions to be made. I will go into more detail later, but for now, here are the first basic questions:

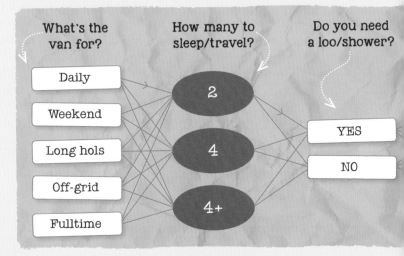

What's the van for?
- Daily
- Weekend
- Long hols
- Off-grid
- Fulltime

How many to sleep/travel?
- 2
- 4
- 4+

Do you need a loo/shower?
- YES
- NO

New versus old

Do you go for new or old? Good question.

A lot of it depends on budget but, when I say old, I don't mean classic versus modern. I mean new brand new versus preloved.

Just FYI: 'classic', according to the HMRC, is anything over 40 years old. That means anything made before 1 January 1981 (at the time of writing) is considered classic and you don't have to pay tax on it. It also doesn't need an MOT.

This means that all Volkswagen Type 2s – that's Bay Windows and Split Screens – and even a few Type 3s (Type 25) are exempt. Also included in this would be early Hymermobils, most Citroën HY vans and most Commer vans.

However, even vans made slightly later in the 1980s may still be considered 'classic', though they don't qualify by HMRC standards.

Brand new vans

Brand new camper vans – or a van that is being converted for you – are wonderful, but costly. So if you have the money you will have a lot of fun choosing all the bits and pieces, options, add-ons and gadgets and widgets. It's a bit like ordering a new car but with two or three more times the number of options. You want memory foam, a heater and an underslung tank? We'll talk about all those things later.

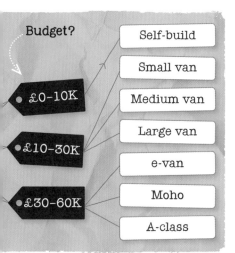

There is no such thing as a standard camper or motorhome, even one that's off the peg. The choices, when buying a motorhome from a dealer, for example, may be as simple as buying an add-on 'winter pack', or it might be much more complicated than that.

Budget?

£0–10K

£10–30K

£30–60K

Self-build

Small van

Medium van

Large van

e-van

Moho

A-class

Even going to a converter and choosing one of their models will lead you down all kinds of roads of possibilities as you'll have to choose a base vehicle, and all the bits and pieces that come with it, before you even get on to your camping set-up.

Buying new: visit a dealer

While I am not advocating wasting anyone's time, I think it's a good plan to visit a big motorhome or camper van dealership to see what's available, what things cost and what your money could buy you if it were no object, even if you are thinking of buying preloved.

If you can also do a factory tour at the same time then you'll get a good insight into the way campers are put together, the work that goes into converting new (or old) campers and the possibilities when it comes to choosing layouts, accessories and your individual specifications.

BUYING OR CONVERTING 'NEW' There are plenty of companies who can source used vans to convert or will convert new vans for you. Obviously this adds another level of complication to the buying process as you need to choose a base vehicle that's specced right from the off.

Choosing the base vehicle can be just as important as choosing the conversion because some base models are more difficult to convert than other models, simply because of the way they are finished. Often, the more basic the better, as it provides a blank canvas.

Advice: talk to the dealer about what you want and what base vehicle they recommend.

Choosing the basic conversion We are about to go through the reasons for choosing different conversions, which will give you an idea of the kind of things you might need to think about to cut down on your choices. However, when you get to see a dealer or converter you'll get even more choices. Many manufacturers sell similar basic models, with each having different accessories and features and the option of add-ons as you go. This is when the sky becomes the limit, with possibilities for WIFI, digital TV, interior lighting options, showers, water tanks and heaters, interior heating, inverters, swivel seat bases and a whole lot more.

Buying preloved

Don't think that buying second hand gets any easier. In fact, I'd say it gets harder. In choosing something that's right for you, be prepared to face a few conundrums and choices, from the type of bed you choose to the type and age of the base vehicle. There are always compromises to be made.

My recommendation: go to as many big dealers, motorhome retailers, VW festivals and conventions as you can. Nose about in as many vehicles as you can. Check out the layouts, seating arrangements and budget and try to identify the vehicle that's perfect for you.

There will be one, all you have to do is find it.

BUYING ADVICE

When you are buying a vehicle, the thing to keep at the back of your mind is 'buyer beware'. That means if it dies or falls apart or doesn't live up to expectations, the only person you can blame, in many cases, is yourself.

However, the law will protect you in some circumstances. If you buy from a dealer then through sale of goods legislation (Sale of Goods Act 1979), you are entitled to expect that any goods you buy are of satisfactory quality. That means they must be of a reasonable quality that a reasonable person could expect, in relation to the way the goods were described, the price and the fact that they were second hand. So, is it fit for purpose? Is it of satisfactory appearance? Is it as described? If not, then you are entitled to a full refund (within a reasonable time period after the sale) but you'll need to demonstrate the goods were not of satisfactory quality at the time of sale.

When you buy privately you do not have so many rights. You can still expect the vehicle to be as described and if it is not, you can sue for compensation. But the best advice here is to be fully aware of what you are buying. Check it over and check it over again. If things go dreadfully wrong, talk to the seller.

Take a mechanic with you when you view If you can, take someone with you who can give the vehicle a good going over when you view any vehicle for the first time. That means looking at the vehicle properly inside and out, underneath and on top. If you are looking at a classic or vintage camper, take a checklist and carefully look at each item in turn.

Follow your instinct

Look at the seller. Observe their body language. How do they seem to you? Honest? Above board? Are they willing to let you give the vehicle a good going over? Does it feel good? If it doesn't, don't let your excitement get the better of you. Take some time to think about it.

Lower your expectations and be pleasantly surprised
You might want it to be perfect, but don't expect it to be so – lower your expectations. If you think it's going to be a crock, then find it isn't, you'll already be on to a winner.

Ask questions
Ask lots of questions about everything. Be relentless. Ask about history, cost of ownership, miles per gallon (mpg), anything you can think of. Get as much info as you can from the seller. And don't be afraid to call up if you think of anything else after you've viewed it.

Look at the log book and history
The history of a vehicle can tell you a lot about how it's been treated. If it has had lots of owners or if there are MOTs missing or bills showing what work has been done, then you'll find out more about it than the owner may be able or willing to tell you. No history doesn't always mean dodgy history, but it could be a sign of something.

Test everything Turn on the gas. Fire up the fridge. Open the cupboards. Pull out the bed. Pop the top. Test everything to check if it works. If things are broken or not working as they should, then you can either use it to negotiate a drop in price or as a reason not to buy. Don't ever feel pressured.

That's it. If it's not right, don't buy it, no matter how pretty it is.

Top tips for searching for your perfect camper

Go to a big motorhome show and see how the big boys do it. There are Caravan, Camping and Motorhome shows all over the UK and Europe. Those at the NEC Birmingham (usually February and October) and Düsseldorf (September) are the biggest. Warners Group also put on shows around the UK.

Expect to see everything from micro campers and the latest in camping technology (eVehicles and more) to huge A-class monsters from Europe's biggest manufacturers.

Go to a VW meet-up if you are looking for anything VW. There are VW shows all over the UK all summer, with the biggest being Busfest and the Volksworld Shows. A visit to the Show and Shine field (where the best vehicles are displayed) may well give you van envy, but there will undoubtedly be countless vehicles for sale. It's a good place to meet converters and suppliers of kit, too.

Rent before you buy. I think this is so important that I have given it a whole section later on. Some people find out very quickly that a camper van is not for them when they rent, even if they find the perfect layout or van. You can save yourself a lot of money this way! Turn to pages 39–41 to read about renting in full.

Go to a large dealership or converter. Here, you'll get an opportunity to look at a lot of vans in one place. There are many to choose from but here are some that I know well.

• Marquis Motorhomes has dealerships in every corner of the UK, with hundreds of models to look at in each location. **www.marquisleisure.co.uk**

• VW Kampers, on the south coast of the UK, sells a vast stock of used Danbury Brazilian VW imports as well as those made in Germany, Australia and South Africa. **www.vwkampers.com**

Join a Facebook group. There are loads of Facebook groups where vans get bought and sold every day. Even if you don't buy one from Facebook (buyer beware) you'll be able to see what people are asking. And the comments are priceless.

Search the Web. There are also lots of places where it is possible to browse camper vans and motorhomes for sale as well as get sound advice. The Caravan and Motorhome Club has a good classifieds section on their website for second-hand motorhomes and bits and pieces, while eBay is a favourite, both for buyers and the odd dodgy seller. Buyer beware.

Search for a classic. The Classic Camper Club concerns itself with other makes beyond VWs, thankfully, although it's tough to get away from them. Take a peek. You may well fall in love yet. **www.classiccamperclub.co.uk**

Read magazines and books, err, like this one. Read *MMM* (*Motorcaravan Motorhome Monthly*), *Camper Van*, *VolksWorld*, *Camper & Bus* and any other specialist magazine and you'll soon find out what's available. Mind-boggling though it may be.

Accost people and be nosy. I love showing people around my camper if they ask politely when I am out and about. So if you see one you like the look of, just ask. The worst they can say is no. But they might show you around and it may be up for sale...

Rust-free VW? Consider an import. VWs from hot countries like Australia and South Africa are often rust free and RHD (right-hand drive). Plenty of companies import them to restore or drive as they are. Imports from California and Mexico for the LHD lovers. See **www.gdaykombis.co.uk**

Things to think about when buying your camper

It can be baffling trying to get to grips with all the different options available to you. There are all kinds of considerations and compromises to think about.

In this section, I have tried to simplify the buying and choosing process into a series of questions to ask yourself. Hopefully, in answering them you'll be able to narrow down the field a bit.

You'll need to think about your budget, your family (now and in the future), the amount of time and love you are prepared to invest and what kind of camping you want to do.

Oh, and how fast you want to travel.

Question 1:	Why do you want or need a camper van/motorhome? > *see* page 19
Question 2:	What will it be used for? > *see* page 20
Question 3:	What's your budget? > *see* page 21
Question 4:	How many do you need to sleep/carry? > *see* page 22
Question 5:	How do you camp? > *see* page 29
Question 6:	What do you need up top? > *see* page 34

WHY DO YOU WANT OR NEED A CAMPER VAN/MOTORHOME?

There is no wrong or right answer to this simple question. Whatever your answer, this will help to define and set out your aims and dreams for the vehicle you hope to own. You define its use and the way you see it. Are you looking for something to cherish, to bring back to life, to take you on the biggest adventures of your life, because you think it's cool, because you are too long in the tooth to camp in discomfort or just because you want to save a few quid?

Is it to own a classic? Yes? That's fine. Be prepared to lavish money and time on your new ride. Lots of it. You'll get looks and envious glances but you'll be driving something quirky and interesting, that's for sure.

Is it to travel the world? Choose an overlander, a 4x4 or something super reliable and as fully equipped as possible. In all likelihood you'll need heating, water tanks, shower and a loo as well as solar and the ability to go off-grid.

Is it to get away every weekend? The camper is the ideal getaway vehicle for weekends. You may not need a loo or shower if you are going to sites and you may not even need solar or huge onboard water tanks. A day van (one with a bed and not much in the way of kitchen equipment) may do. A van with a removable kitchen pod may be useful, especially if you want to use the vehicle during the week for something else.

Is it because you want to save money on accommodation? Yes, you can save on hotels, but when you consider the cost of purchase and of ownership upkeep (especially if it's older) then you may not end up saving a huge amount, unless you sleep in it a lot.

Is it because you want to carry sports gear or equipment? If you are doing sports such as triathlons, surfing and kayaking, even snowboarding, and need to travel to do it, a van or motorhome can be perfect. Some bigger motorhomes have garages for kit like inflatable SUPs, bikes and even motorbikes, while some vans have huge cargo areas where the rear bed lifts up enough to fit in bikes and kit. Rear-mounted bike carriers can be limited on weight, especially when it comes to ebikes, and for bikes that need to be cocooned.

Kayaks are more difficult on bigger vans as you may need ladders to get them up. If you are travelling solo then you may need specialist racks so that you can load a kayak on your own. See **www.karitek.co.uk** for kayak and canoe mounting racks for tall vehicles.

Thule make all kinds of racks and ladders for tall vans and motorhomes. **www.thule.co.uk**

Is it because you still want to camp but don't want to give up your comforts? Lots of people come to camper vans and motorhomes from camping or because they like their home comforts too much to camp under canvas. You can decide what level of comfort you go for but, basically, anything goes! If all you want is a dry bed you can drive around, then a camper may be enough. If you want space and all mod cons, a motorhome may be the way to go.

WHAT WILL IT BE USED FOR?

This might sound like a silly question, but it's not. You need to decide whether your van or motorhome will be used exclusively for camping or will be a daily driver too. If it's to be a vehicle you use to pop to the shops as well as camp in, then I would suggest a smaller camper van might be best, simply because you will be able to find a parking space for it more easily. Large vans like Boxer and Ducato vans are wide and not so easy to park. If you opt for a long wheelbase van then it will be longer than one space, too, which makes everyday driving difficult.

It's the same with motorhomes. Some are more than 7ft (2.1m) wide and many are longer than the average car parking space.

Also, think about where you will be going. If you like to tour the narrow lanes of Cornwall, your needs will be different from someone who intends to navigate the open roads of Europe.

On top of that, motorhomes and campers that only go on outings are likely to have fewer miles on the clock, be less worn and may well have a higher resale value.

WHAT'S YOUR BUDGET?

Sorry, but this is the nitty gritty. Your budget will decide everything, from the age to the interior to the condition, mileage and number of owners. It also comes back to the 'why' question.

It's easy to spend a small fortune on a camper and you could do this just as easily with a modern camper as with a classic from the 1960s.

It all depends on how far you want to go. It's worthwhile totting up the running costs, too. Keeping an old camper on the road can be just as costly as buying it in the first place.

Then again, it is possible to self-build from an older, cheaper vehicle for just a few thousand pounds. It all depends how far you want to go and what kind of carpentry skills you possess.

How much is it going to cost you?

Model	£££££s
2021 VW T6 California Ocean (4 berth)	57K–76K
2021 VW Crafter Grand California 680 (2 berth)	76K–90K
2021 Danbury Surf: (4 berth) pop top, no kitchen	46K–66K
VW Bay Window Type 2	5K–40K+
A-class motorhome (second hand)	10K–60K
New Fiat Ducato base model	25K–40K
Nissan e-NV200 camper (2 berth)	59K
Second-hand Ford Tourneo base van	10K–40K
Cost of professional conversion	10K–40K

4 HOW MANY DO YOU NEED TO SLEEP/ CARRY?

Another fundamental question. If it's just you then it's easy. Life is so much simpler. You just throw it all in the back and enjoy living the way you want to.

Two is easy, too, as you kind of hope there's some sort of agreement between you that makes the sleeping arrangements amicable and comfortable. Most camper vans – except perhaps the micro campers – will sleep at least two. It just gets a little more difficult when you go beyond that.

The fact is that everyone is different and everyone's needs are different. And every family, or group, changes as time goes on. Kids don't stay kids forever. They have a tricky habit of growing up, getting bigger and growing out of bunk beds, hammocks and high-top sleeping platforms.

CAMPER VANS

Couples and small kids For two-berth camper vans it is possible to add hammocks that fit across the front seat and fasten to the A pillar and window pillars, or that slip over swivel seats. These have a weight restriction of around 50kg (110lb) so are only really suitable for younger kids. They can also be used for storage, which can be useful when you want to fling off your clothes and dive into bed (and find all your clothes again the next morning).

Families with bigger kids Unless you intend to use a pup tent or sleep in an awning (*see* pages 158–160 for more) then you'll need to look at four-berth campers.

Many modern small van conversions include pop tops with a large double 'upstairs'. This is by far the most popular style of conversion for smaller vans as it adds two extra berths for a relatively small cost (£2,000–3,000) in a van that can be driven every day.

Larger vans and families Many larger van conversions are built for families and have four berths in all kinds of combinations, usually in long wheelbase models. Check out the following models for a family of four:

- Auto-Sleeper Fairford
- Auto-Trail Tribute
- Hymer Free
- Globecar Summit
- WildAx Solaris

Lots of European campers also offer four berths with the addition of a fixed bed in the rear, but this can restrict the living space up front, on the assumption that you will spend more time outside than in during the average European summer.

Hymer make a Fiat Ducato based camper that has a pop top and sleeps four, with the added advantage of having a shower and full kitchen, plus a fixed bed and inside garage.

Currently, the only small classic VW that can sleep more than four is the Super Viking, which can sleep six. However, and this is something to watch for, the Super Viking only seats five. So who's the extra one?

NOTE: In vehicles manufactured after 2006, passengers must travel in designated travel seats. That means you can only travel with the same number of people as there are designated seats, irrespective of the number of berths.

There's more important information about seat belt law on pages 148–149.

MOTORHOMES

Motorhomes and larger conversions are a lot easier. In fact, many of them are aimed at the family market, with lounge areas that convert into beds or even drop-down beds that enable you all to sleep at different levels.

If you intend to camp in the winter with more than two people then a larger van or motorhome will be infinitely more comfortable, since pop tops have little in the way of insulation.

More than four If you are looking at sleeping more than four then you will need to consider a motorhome or a bespoke build that can fit you all in.

There are plenty of standard models of motorhomes that will safely seat and sleep six comfortably. Usually this will include two above the cab, two in the dining area and two in the rear 'master bedroom'.

SLEEPING LAYOUTS

By now you will know that different campers and motorhomes have different layouts. The layout will always affect the way you live and sleep in any camper, even in the most spacious of vans. Some work well, some are OK while the kids are small, some are perfect for two but awful with four.

Camper Van

THE THREE-QUARTER WIDTH ROCK AND ROLL This is the 'industry standard' nowadays. It's the layout that's lasted because it's the most practical, giving a healthy compromise between space to sleep and storage space. It applies as much to vintage campers as it does to modern campers and is the adopted style of the T5 California, among many others. Some r'n'r beds are safer than others (*see* pages 91–93 for more).

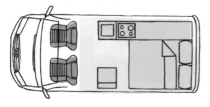

THE FULL-WIDTH ROCK AND ROLL
If you need sleeping and chilling space, this is a good layout to go for. However, the compromise is storage space, as your units will be at the front. In older vans, it gives you the option of having three seats with belts in the back, and the two inertia reel belts.

REAR KITCHEN/ SHOWER

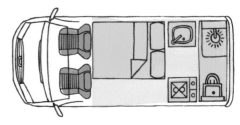

This is a popular layout for couples who like smaller campers but don't want to give up the indoor plumbing. In early models it allowed for a rear kitchen, and in modern conversions it allows for a kitchen plus loo and even shower arrangement. Offers two single beds using the front swivel seats.

Van Conversion
REAR BUNKS WITH FRONT DOUBLE

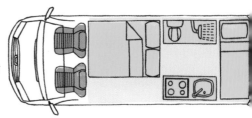

Rear bunks are great if your van is wide enough to fit them in. However, unless you are driving something that's over 6ft (1.8m) wide, it might not be much good for grown-ups.

DROP-DOWN BED

This is a bed that drops down from the ceiling over a living area or lower beds to add two more berths. Very useful in large vans to maximise space.

REAR 'LOUNGE'

This type of layout is only really possible in larger vans and van-derived motorhomes that have space enough for two side-facing bench seats in the back. These then turn into a big double bed. The greatest advantage of these is having good space and the ability to open the rear doors to the outside. However, having a galley kitchen and shower in the middle of the camper can compromise the living space.

Motorhome And Large Van Conversion

FIXED BEDS

In recent years there has been a trend towards the fixed bed. That's a bed that stays made up during the day. In large van conversions these are often able to swing upwards out of the way to allow bikes and kit to be stored while driving, while also keeping the bed made! Some conversions put the fixed bed above the garage at the back, giving lots of storage. Useful in vans over 6ft (1.8m) wide. VW's Grand California does this: it is a 'typical European' layout.

Motorhome

FIXED BEDS AND MASTER BEDROOM

In larger motorhomes the space is there to make master bedrooms that have fixed beds over garages. They may be separated from the living area by the bathroom, with a shower on one side and loo on the other.

OVERCAB BEDS, LUTON STYLE

A-class motorhomes and coach-built motorhomes often have overcab bunks. They are useful if you want extra storage, as sleeping bags, pillows, etc can then be slung upstairs out of the way during the day. It also leaves space for more beds downstairs.

Classic Van

VIKING SPACEMAKER

The Viking Spacemaker roof was launched in the early 1974 and represented something novel and innovative at the time, which was an overhanging roof that could sleep three or four adults in a circular ring of beds around the central roof opening. They are somewhat of a rarity today but much loved.

HOW DO YOU CAMP?

We all camp the same don't we? We turn up, cook, hang out, sleep, wake and do it all again. Well, yes, but no. Just as all camper vans are different, all camping experiences are different, too. If you know the types of places you are going, and the type of camping you intend to do, then it can really help you to decide what type of van is going to be right for you.

There is a lot more about campsites and camping later on, but, for the moment let's discuss camping styles and how they might affect your choice of camper van.

Glamorous camping This term came into being a little while ago and it's now become the new thing. But what does it mean? Glamping is a bastardisation of 'glamour' and 'camping' designed to attract those who like their comforts while doing something that perhaps isn't always such a glamorous activity.

What does your average glamper drive? Something glamorous, obviously, probably vintage, maybe even a little quirky. That means it needs to be some kind of a classic.

- Space, for lounging around glamorously
- Shower and toilet
- Kitchen, for preparing glamorous snacks and Italian classics
- Retro looks and styling to make it everso groovy
- Lots of comforts and space so it's not like camping at all

What you need: A retrotastic 1980s A-class? Maybe. Perhaps a Karmann Gypsy.

Festival camping I don't know what type of festivals you are used to, but those that I have been to tend to be mucky affairs, with madness outside and a lot of rain. So the perfect festival camper van needs to be a private space where you can get away from the chaos to reapply the lip gloss before venturing out again for more. It doesn't really have to be anything other than dry, comfortable and warm, perhaps with a fridge for keeping a few beers cool.

- Porta Potti, to save late-night trips to the portaloos
- Fridge, for keeping a few beers on ice
- Cooker, for putting on a brew first thing in the morning
- A very comfortable bed, for crashing out
- Good curtains (or blackouts), for keeping out nosey neighbours

A VW classic will make you feel all cool and whatnot, but a 4WD Bongo might stand a better chance of getting you out of there once the fat lady has sung.

What you need: An overlander with chunky tyres for grip in the mud, or an all-wheel drive VW or T25 Synchro to guarantee you'll get out of there. 4WD all the way.

Touring park camping This is the kind of camping most of us will be used to. Touring parks are the kind of campsites that have a little of everything. You can expect electric hook-up (EHU), hardstanding pitches, clean toilets and showers (we hope), plus all mod cons. There may also be a shop. Basically, it's a very safe way of camping, with everything laid on.

- Kitchenette
- Beds
- Electric unit (if you want to charge mobiles, tablets, etc.)
- Awning, if you need more space to spread out
- The kitchen sink, for a good quality family holiday

What you need: Any camper will do, to be honest. It all depends on the level of comfort you expect, the amount of space you need and the number of you. Most campsites will allow you to add to your space by putting up an awning or a pup tent (*see* pages 158–160 for more).

Small site camping Small sites are the non-corporate sites where it can be a bit rough and ready. These are the type of sites that appeal to the independently minded camper. They may be in a farmer's field or just in a great spot. Any type of camper van might be perfect, although bigger vans and large 'units' might struggle a little if there is no hardstanding. If your van relies on having electric, then these kind of sites might not always be right. They're often without electric, shops or much in the way of glamorous comfort. Best kind, IMHO.

- Capable of being independent of electric
- Kitchen and BBQ
- Fire pit (if allowed), for genuine 'out there' feeling
- Awning or pup tent (for leaving gear), if you go out and about

What you need: Anything goes, although big motorhomes might not last too long if electric is an issue and access to hardstanding is unavailable.

Stealth camping As the name suggests, stealth camping is the type of camping you do under the radar. Often in towns, pub car parks or at the side of the road, but done in such a way as to avoid detection. The stealth camper van needs to be unassuming, without accoutrements (on the outside) and, for all intents and purposes, look like a standard van.

- No windows, or blacked-out windows
- Whatever you need inside – no one can see in anyway
- No bikes, roof racks or any kind of outside stuff
- No awnings

What you need: This is when the 'white van man'-type van comes into its own. Suits any home conversions without windows, and converted tin top VWs without windows. Perfect for an ex-AA Type 4, blacked-out T5, large Sprinter or any large van.

Wild camping This is camping off-grid, out there, away from it all. This is where the camper van comes into its own for my money. You've got everything you really require – heat, light, comfort – so there's no need for any of the extra glampy comforts like electricity or showers. If there's no loo you might have to take a spade or a Porta Potti.

- Cooking gear
- Porta Potti
- Spade
- Fire pit/BBQ
- Solar shower

What you need: A small van for getting down little lanes, plus water, solar and a Porta Potti so you don't have to despoil the countryside. A big van with everything on board. A motorhome.

Aire camping This is camping in designated spaces and particularly applies in Europe. The rules of aire camping dictate that you must not spread out beyond your camper, and so tables and chairs and hammocks cannot be put out. If you carry a lot of kit, camping on aires can be difficult as everything needs to be packed away, even in night mode. With a family of four in a small camper, things can get tight.

- Perfect for bigger vans and motorhomes
- Need to be self-contained
- Some aires have toilets
- Some hook-ups available
- Stay for 24–48 hours max

What you need: Again, lots of campers will be perfect for aire camping, although day vans might struggle if they rely on the extra space from a pup tent or awning to camp.

Britstop/Passion camping Passion sites are camping places available to self-contained motorhomes and campers at places like vineyards, farms, *auberges* and restaurants. Like aire camping, you need to be self-contained as many sites won't have toilets, taps or electricity. Britstops are the same but in the UK, and largely pubs and farm shops.

- Free but be prepared to spend on a meal or goods
- Must be self-contained
- Suitable for bigger motorhomes and self-contained campers

What you need: Big motorhomes are fine for these sorts of stops, but you need to be self-contained and containable. If you can camp without toilets, water or electricity then you'll love Passion sites and Britstops.

QUESTION
6 WHAT DO YOU NEED UP TOP?

TYPES OF ROOF STYLES AND WHAT THEY MEAN TO THE AVERAGE CAMPER

One of the first decisions you're going to face when you consider a camper is what sort of top it's got – or what sort of top you are going to need. There are various options to consider and each has advantages and drawbacks.

Tin top This is a standard (low) metal roof on any van or camper. In the case of a VW it'll be a van that still has its original roof.

• **Who wants a tin top?** Tin top campers are great for couples or singles and families who are happy to camp using a pup tent for kids or extra guests. In smaller vans, having a tin top usually means having just one double bed in the back. Tin tops are also useful for people who want to camp stealthily in a vehicle that looks more like a works van than a camper.

• **What's so good about a tin top?** The advantages of having a tin top are that it won't leak, it is more streamlined (and arguably more fuel efficient) and it retains the original lines.

However, the disadvantage is that it'll make standing up impossible. So everything will need to be done sitting down, cooking included.

High top vans Small campers often have high roofs fitted, whereas larger vans are more often than not high roofed by default. Sprinters and Crafters are mostly made in high-roof versions.

High roofs on smaller vans are either added on after manufacture by camper conversion companies or are specified at the factory.

• **Who wants a high top?** High tops on smaller vans have one major advantage over other conversions or vans: they enable you to stand up. It might not seem a significant addition but it can make a huge difference, especially when it comes to cooking.

High tops often have enough space in the roof for a secondary bed or 'upstairs' for small children or small adults, something that instantly turns your two-berth camper into a four-berth vehicle.

• **What's so good about a high top?** As well as the standing up business, the high-top roof offers space for storage and means you can stow bedding, clothes, kit and all the stuff you like to carry in the roof – leaving the 'downstairs' tidy – as you drive.

• **Why don't we all drive high tops?** High tops can be tricky to drive in side winds. They also produce more wind resistance than more aerodynamic shapes, which can affect the speed and fuel consumption.

Also, they can be a problem at some beauty spots, supermarkets, car parks and places where there are height restrictions. A standard smaller van with a pop top is likely to stand around 6 1/2ft (2m) tall – and will fit under most height barriers.

Pop tops The pop top is the way many camper van builders add extra sleeping space without compromising the lines too much. The original roof is cut out and replaced with a fibreglass roof that either pops up on struts or hinges at one side. This then forms a roof tent with bellows made from cloth or vinyl and, in some cases, from solid panels.

• **Who wants a pop top?** Pop tops and side elevating roofs are fantastic for families as they double the sleeping capacity of an ordinary pop top van, adding options of either a double up top or bunks.

They also offer standing room for cooking and living for people who want extra space when they park up.

• **What's so good about a pop top?** Pop tops are great for adding space without adding height. They will alter the profile of the van but not significantly, like a high top will. Pop tops can also be retrofitted to most vans, which makes them perfect for the home conversion market. Pop tops will add to the value of a converted van.

• **Why wouldn't you want a pop top?** The pop top, while creating space, only does so when parked up with the top popped. So they are great for turning a standard day van or tin top into a four-berth camper van, but useless if you want to increase the luggage-carrying capacity of your van.

Pop tops won't always carry roof racks (although many will) so it's worth considering this if you need to carry boards, bikes, top boxes or any of that stuff.

Carrying gear/boards/kayaks/toys

WHY YOUR TOYS SHOULD DETERMINE HOW YOUR CAMPER ROLLS

If you are like me then you will need to consider your toys in your choice of vehicle. In fact, I would say it really is one of the most important factors when you come to select your vehicle. What you need to carry will dictate everything, especially if it's bikes and boards or kayaks.

BIKE RACKS There are lots of bike racks on the market and there are a few ways of carrying them. Tow bar-mounted racks can often carry four full-sized bikes – and can carry an awful lot more weight – while rear-mounted racks depend on the shape of the vehicle.

Motorhome racks that bolt on to the rear panel of the van itself can often carry more weight than those that attach to the rear doors of a large van. In fact, large van racks are often designed to carry just two bikes.

Roof-mounted racks also depend on the ability to carry a roof rack or the ability to be able to get access to the roof (on bigger vans).

It is an important consideration if you are a family of four and want to travel with all your bikes. Lots of bike racks, especially for older vans, will only carry a couple of bikes. This is down to the fact that the racks sit on the rear tailgate so can't carry too much weight. Later models have fewer issues and can carry more weight.

If a rear-mounted carrier isn't an option then consider a tow bar-mounted version. You'll need a tow bar for this, obviously, which is another consideration as most vehicles don't come fitted as standard with them. They can also get in the way of rear barn doors!

ROOF MOUNTING YOUR BIKES This is pretty simple – if you can fit roof bars to your van. But some pop tops won't take roof bars unless you drill them because the profile of the pop top restricts access to the guttering. Also, consider the weight of the bikes on your pop top. And don't forget about them when you go under low bridges.

SURFBOARDS/KAYAKS/SUPS/WINDSURFERS Carrying surfboards is pretty straightforward if you can fit roof bars on your camper. The only potential issue is security, in which case you can invest in lockable straps or make sure your boards are locked away in the van when you aren't with it.

Westfalia supplies special brackets to fit roof bars on its pop tops, while products like Camper Van Culture's Load Rings will allow you to strap boards down to pop tops without fitting specific roof bars.

If you are considering a high top then you may need to think about mounting J bars on the side of your roof to carry boards. Some of these will sit on the gutter and fix to the roof itself, while others will have to be adapted to bolt on to the roof itself.

LARGE VANS AND MOTORHOMES Mounting gear on the roof gets harder the taller the vehicle, and often means the addition of ladders. Telescopic ladders store away easily and mean that security is less of a risk for gear on the roof. Another downside is the added height to the van. Make sure you know what height you reach fully loaded – low bridges may be a challenge.

For solo travellers, side-loading roof bars can be invaluable for kayaks and boards. They enable you to load a kayak on to the rack and then load the rack on to the top of the van.

RENTING A CAMPER

Rent before you buy. This is the sagest piece of advice I am ever going to give you if you are looking for a camper van. For some people the reality of life in a tin box doesn't live up to the hype.

I hear from camper rental companies that occasionally they get camper vans brought back before the due date by campers with tired eyes and mournful faces, who drop the keys back on the rental desk with a sigh, claiming it just wasn't for them.

It happens. Some people want more than what the camper van can offer. If you've known indoor plumbing and deeply filled hotel baths with pools and waiters and views overlooking the sea, you might be just a little disappointed with your campsite. It's understandable.

But hey, better to find out when you are just a few hundred quid down than when you have just handed over your life savings.

My advice? Rent a van for a week, a weekend, a night. It really doesn't matter. Once you have parked up, got the kettle on and settled down for the night you'll know. If, after a week you still love it, start saving.

HOW TO AVOID A RENTAL CAMPER VAN

DISASTER Choose wisely. Rent with a company that is well established, with back-up plans if things go wrong.

- Go with a rental company that can provide you with a back-up vehicle if things go wrong. Ask questions. Make sure it will look after you properly. Does it have roadside assistance? What will happen if you break down?
- Get prices from lots of companies. Don't go for the cheapest quote (as with everything in life).
- Do not overpack. Camper vans are small. So take the least you think you can get away with. I hear that lots of customers take everything – and I mean everything – when they rent a camper for the first time. This will only end in misery as you will have to move everything each time you want to go to bed or make a brew. Take less, enjoy more.
- Make sure the rental has a bike rack or roof racks to carry bikes, boards and any of that stuff. Double-check.
- When the sun shines, make hay. By this I mean stop and take a few minute to smell the coffee. Park up. Put your feet up. Read a book. Enjoy the moment.
- Never underestimate the power of a good brew in a tense situation. Get the kettle on.
- Kick back and slack. Stop haring around. You wouldn't hit 60 if you tried so don't try. Learn to live at the pace of the van, not at the pace you're used to. Nothing wrong with underachieving. Achieve nothing.
- Make a plan and stick to it – but don't be overambitious. The freedom of the open road is all very well but a little planning goes a long way. Go and see stuff you have wanted to for ages.
- Book into a really good campsite. Don't settle for anything less than something really special. Disappointing campsites can kill your expectations stone dead. If the weather is looking iffy, book into a campsite with a bar, indoor pool, sheltered BBQ area or restaurant.

Rental companies

There are plenty of companies around, with new outfits springing up all the time. You only have to do a quick search on the web to realise that. As such, companies come and go, and, as often with these things, some may be better than others. So here are my limited recommendations. They're purely personal and based on what I know. It doesn't mean others aren't also excellent, but I have no experience to back this up.

SOUTH

O'CONNORS CAMPERS has a fleet of 15 camper vans, including relatively new VW T5 Californias. They are one of the UK's oldest rental companies and have a huge amount of experience, in-house mechanics and a really good way of working. They're lovely folks too. Perfect for trips west.

Highlands, Old Road, High Street, Okehampton, EX20 1SP
01837 659599
penny@oconnors
campers.co.uk
www.oconnorscamper.co.uk

NORTH

DEESIDE CLASSIC CAMPERS is relatively new but its campers are a cut above. Claire, who owns the company, has big ideas and demands rigorous standards from her campers. As such, they are immaculately decked out, beautifully prepared and well maintained. If you want to see the highlands, this is the way.

Crann Dearg, Drumhead, Finzean, Aberdeenshire, AB31 6PB
01330 850555
office@deesideclassic
campers.com
www.deesideclassic
campers.com

Part Two

BEFORE YOU GO

It's Friday. The forecast is good.

The promise of a long, hot weekend under the stars, a few nights at the coast, a week in France or a month in southern Spain is just a drive away. Ferry's booked. Passports found, checked and packed. Fairy lights sought and marshmallows bought.

You're almost there.

Ready?

Have you remembered to pack the toothbrushes? Did you get the travel cover? Did you get another bottle of that green loo stuff? Have you booked the campsite? Do I need my waterproofs? What's the best way to avoid the traffic? Where are we going to get gas? Can I bring my surfboard and bike?

This section is called 'Before you go' because it's about the stuff you might need to sort out on Wednesday, or Thursday at the very latest, to make your transition from home to holiday as seamless as possible. Even if you are just going to the beach down the road for a night out you'll still need to do some preparation for a stress-free getaway. Unless, like on page 58, you're all set to go, right here, right now, as the feeling takes you. That's more like it.

Spending time on preparation might go against everything we hold dear about the free-as-a-bird van lifestyle, but a little always goes a long, long way.

You'll thank me when you turn the key and head off, knowing you've got everything you need on board.

Or have you?

(Your quick checklist is on page 53.)

DRIVING

CAN YOU DRIVE IT? PAYLOADS, WEIGHTS, LICENCES

Your driving licence and motorhomes

Driving licences, and the categories of vehicles they allow you to drive, have changed over the years. It's relevant for camper van and motorhome drivers because it will mean you may need to take an additional test if you were born after 1 January 1997. Anyone born before then is entitled to drive what is now known as C1 or C1+E categories. This will allow you to drive a vehicle up to 7.5 tonnes or up to 12 tonnes with a trailer (handy if you want to tow a car, for example). Some people call it the 'grandparent privilege'.

For those of you who passed their test after 1 January 1997 you will have to take an additional test to gain your C1 certification and may only drive vehicles up to and including 3.5 tonnes (in total). This includes lots of vehicles, so don't despair! A VW T6 weighs around 2,800kg while a Type 2 (Bay Window) weighs in at just over 1,100kg. A long wheel-based van like the Ducato weighs in at about 3,000kg.

At the age of 70 you will need to renew your licence every three years. This can be done online.

Weights and payloads

The licence you hold has a bearing on the type of van or motorhome you can drive, governed by weight. And this is defined by something called the maximum authorised mass (MAM), which is the total of the kerb weight and the payload.

The unladen weight is the weight of the vehicle when it's not carrying anything, including passengers, fuel and in the case of a van, the weight of any water or supplies.

The payload is the amount of weight that the vehicle is allowed to carry (including passengers, fuel and supplies) before it reaches the MAM. Anything over that will mean the vehicle is travelling illegally and, more importantly perhaps, unsafely.

The MAM should be listed in your owner's manual or shown on the vehicle (on a plate or sticker). The MAM and weight in service (kerb weight) should also be noted on your V5C registration document.

THE WEIGHT OF YOUR CONVERSION When driving a van or motorhome it's important to also consider the weight of the conversion, including the bed, furniture and everything that's permanently included in the van. This, of course, will affect the payload and mean that you may not be able to carry all that stuff! The only way of checking is to take your vehicle to a weighbridge (if you are home converting or have bought a conversion and not been given the weight by the converter).

CHECK THE PAYLOAD When you are buying a van or motorhome, check the payload with the manufacturer. Some motorhomes have a payload of as little as 300kg, which, when you consider the average Joe weighs 60kg, isn't that much! Check what the payload needs to include. Manufacturers may well not include the weight of gas canisters and leisure batteries.

CONSIDER THE AXLE WEIGHT Your vehicle will have an axle weight, too, which is the maximum weight either of your axles can carry. The payload must be distributed evenly between the axles, which is a danger in motorhomes with a rear garage.

Tips for reducing travelling weight

• Check your licence allows you to drive the vehicle (especially if you are renting).

• Always travel with your water tank empty, or with just enough for a cuppa at most.

• Shop when you get there (it will help to save fuel and will help you to contribute to the local economy). It's surprising how much food weighs!

• Pack lightly and make a rough calculation of your payload before you go.

Know your dimensions

How high is your van? How high is it with the kayaks on the roof? How wide is it? How long is it?

These are important questions. And if you end up asking them of yourself as you hurtle towards that low bridge, the narrow one-way street or that teeny tiny parking space, it may be too late.

Tip

Write the dimensions of your vehicle, laden and unladen on a piece of paper and pop it behind your sun visor. Remind yourself of it when you need it – instead of ducking and hoping for the best.

Get proper cover

No book on camping and travel would be complete without a mention of travel cover. Whether you are accident-prone or not, it is an essential piece of kit whenever you hit the road, especially overseas.

FOLLOWING FCO ADVICE In recent years we have been witness (and sometimes victims) to the government's advice on foreign travel. The rule to remember is that, when the government advises against all but essential travel to a country, it means your travel insurance will, most likely, not cover you for travel in that country. This means your possessions and, more worryingly, your health is not covered. It is possible to get cover but, traditionally, this has been the reserve of the war correspondents and business people doing stuff in war zones and unsafe areas. Following the Covid-19 pandemic, all that changed and countries with an unusually high infection rate became targets for the FCO. As well as meaning your insurance may not be valid it also means you have to quarantine when you get home.

VEHICLE COVER What if you break down while towing in Turin? Or clap out in Clacton? Would you know how to get yourself home? Or would you leave it to chance and hope for the best? The sensible camper would make sure the vehicle is roadworthy when they set off (obviously) but would also have a plan B tucked away somewhere (usually in the back of the wallet) that would enable them to summon their roadside assistance provider at the touch of a few buttons. Some services will get you home, put you up, talk to local garages and even send drivers out to meet you if things go wrong.

And don't forget that if you break a windscreen or lose a wheel, you'll be losing your transport AND your house all in one fell swoop. So best get cover that will understand.

The Caravan and Motorhome Club's Red Pennant service does all that for their members – with the added benefit of the fact that they know what you're like. **www.caravanclub.co.uk**

PERSONAL INSURANCE OK, so the unit is covered. Who is covering you? Personal travel insurance is another vital part of your camping kit, especially if you travel abroad. Medical bills can soar into the thousands for people who break things or get cuts and bruises while abroad, with bills for more serious conditions spiralling out of control – into the hundreds of thousands in many places. Medical care isn't cheap.

Travel insurance will cover all the other replaceable bits – like luggage, paperwork and gadgets – but will also provide you with the peace of mind you only get from knowing that you will be well taken care of if something happens to your health.

TRAVEL INSURANCE TIPS

- Always check the small print.
- Make sure that you are aware of what your policy will and won't cover before you go.
- If your policy covers a vehicle, make sure it's the right one!
- Declare all medical conditions before you travel.
- If you take medication, always carry a copy of your prescription so you can explain the presence of drugs in your luggage without any fuss.
- If you take medication, take enough with you to last the trip, as drugs can be expensive abroad compared to at home.
- Always declare your medical conditions, as insurers won't pay out if you neglect to mention something and it leads to a claim.
- Be aware that being under the influence of drink or drugs can invalidate claims (*see* next section).
- Make sure your vehicle is adequately maintained as that could also invalidate cover if you haven't taken care of it.
- Remember that your vehicle is also your home so make sure your cover includes hotel stays or alternative accommodation if your van becomes unusable. This is essential for older vans as parts can take days to arrive sometimes – even a broken windscreen can put you out of action for a while.

The end of the EHIC

EU citizens are entitled to carry a European Health Insurance Card (EHIC) while travelling in Europe. This entitles them to the same free healthcare that citizens of that country would automatically receive. While this is OK for people visiting the UK, where healthcare is largely free at the point of care (for now), it is a different matter for people travelling to other countries. Why? Because in some countries, healthcare is not free, with private clinics working alongside government clinics. In some places you may have to pay for an ambulance while in others you may be required to pay for prescriptions or to see a doctor.

What does this mean? If you are from an EU country, always carry your EHIC. If you are from the UK, your EHIC may not be valid after 1 January 2021 and so you will have to get decent travel insurance to avoid huge bills if you get ill.

Travelling with dogs, cats and ferrets (but not at the same time)

Motorhomes make perfect homes for travelling pets and there are plenty of you who travel with your furry friends. It makes a lot of sense because it's familiar, it's relatively easy and means companionship. For people on their own it also means an extra level of security (although ferrets are, apparently, the ones to watch when it comes to security).

Please remember:

- Dogs die in hot vans. Unless you have air con and can guarantee your pet will be OK, don't leave them alone in a vehicle on a hot day.
- Dogs and ferrets aren't always welcome in restaurants, museums, art galleries and tourist attractions. Cats even less so. Your trip will have to revolve around them to a certain extent if you are to avoid abandoning them.
- Some countries require a dog to wear a muzzle on public transport and some breeds may require them more often. Check with the country you are travelling to.
- For fussy dogs, you might need to take their favourite food with you if it's not available in the country you are visiting.

PET PASSPORTS POST BREXIT A pet passport allowed UK-based owners to take their dogs, cats and ferrets to Europe until January 2021. However, it has since become a little more complicated and will, more than likely involve the following:

1 Your pet must be microchipped and vaccinated against rabies.
2 Your pet must have a blood sample taken at least 30 days after its primary rabies vaccination, which will be sent to an EU-approved blood testing laboratory.
3 After three months you may travel, as long as the test is positive, with a copy of the test results in an Animal Health Certificate (AHC).

As long as you keep your pet's rabies vaccinations up to date, you will not need to get repeat blood tests for repeat trips to the EU.

You must also take your pet to a vet no more than 10 days before travel to update your AHC. You'll need your pet's microchipping date,

vaccination history and a successful rabies antibody blood test result.
Your pet's AHC will be valid for:

- 10 days after the date of issue for entry into the EU
- Onward travel within the EU for four months after the date of issue
- Re-entry to Great Britain for four months after the date of issue

Your pet will need a new health certificate for each trip to the EU.
Note: The above information is from **gov.uk**.

TRAVELLING SAFELY WITH YOUR PETS The Highway
Code states that dogs must be suitably restrained so they cannot distract
you or cause injury to you or them if you have to stop quickly. This means
having a harness or a dog cage (that's properly secured) in the van.

In addition, if you have an accident with an unrestrained dog in the
car your insurance may be invalid. You may also face huge fines and
points on your licence for driving without due care.

CHECKING IN ON YOUR PET Thanks to technology it is now
possible to check in on your pet while you're away from your motorhome
using wi-fi, apps and CCTV cameras. Some technology also allows you
to offer treats and start two-way conversations with the pet while you are
away. That said, leaving an animal in a vehicle when it's too hot or too
cold can end tragically. Make the right call.

THE SECRETS OF HAPPY CAMPING

Make a list (or lists)

This book is full of lists. Each section has one. Why? Because they are useful and help to focus the mind on what is important. However, it is also vitally important to remember that lists have to be given an order of importance to make them useful.

If you are the kind of person who cannot travel without stuff, put the stuff on your list. But do remember to debate the importance of any item before they go on the list, not once they are in the van. By then it will be too late and you'll risk travelling in an overcrowded van or discarding the wrong stuff in a fit of overpacking frustration.

To this end, it may help to separate lists into lists, so that you can tell the difference between 'absolutely vital' and 'nice to have'.

Note: Lists may also be location dependent meaning, for example, that if you go somewhere without shops, restaurants or bars, that you might need to pack supplies of food.

LIST 1. Cannot travel without to avoid catastrophe.
   Include: bedding, clothes, prescriptions, insurance, money.
LIST 2. Can do without if pushed but better to have.
   Include: maps, levelling chocks, hoses.
LIST 3. Stuff you wish you had once or twice on a trip.
   Include: binoculars, running shoes, card games.
LIST 4. Luxury items that you only take when you know there's room.
   Include: smart clothes, biscuits.

One man's meat...

Please remember that my examples are based on how I feel about things. It'll be different for everyone. Reference books, binoculars, cameras and all kinds of other stuff are of different importance to different people. The point is that working out what should have priority is vital. If you'd die in a ditch without your Hawaiian shirt before you'd take a pillow, be my guest. It's your party.

Essential camping kit

What do you need? Ultimately it's up to you, but here are some very useful tips for things to pack.

Your quick checklist:

- Clothes
- Food
- Wash gear (*see* pages 57–58)
- Cooking equipment (*see* pages 60–64)
- First aid kit (*see* page 57)
- Van infrastructure (hoses, pegs, fridge, loo, etc.)
- Sleeping gear (*see* pages 99–102)

Anything else, really, is non-essential, although it might seem like it. However, as someone who would consider a surfboard and wetsuit to be among the essentials, I understand that sometimes life demands more than just eating, sleeping and being warm.

ACCESSORIES: WILL THEY MAKE CAMPING EASIER?

Some bits of camping gear are, as we have established, essential. Wet weather gear if you're off to the Hebrides, pegs for the awning, that kind of thing. However, there are a lot of items that will help to make life easier, will give you a better night's sleep or will help to make your space more effective.

There is a lot of camping gadgetry out there. It's like any other massive industry in the respect that there are always innovations and new products for you to splurge your hard-earned cash on. Some of them, inevitably, will be a bit gimmicky, like a musical pillow or a blow-up gadget chair, but it's up to you to decide if they are must-haves and if you have the space to carry them. The list, inevitably, is short, because your van should provide you with basic cooking, washing, dining and sleeping facilities. Anything else is just being greedy.

AN AXE If you need to make kindling, chop logs or generally make any kind of fire, you're going to need one of these. I have a favourite, a lightweight, double-edged billhook that's fantastic for making kindling, if a bit light for dropping trees.

Note: Do not chop trees to make wood for your fire! Only ever burn deadwood, driftwood or logs you bring yourself.

FIRE STEEL Sometimes you lose your matches. Sometimes they get soggy. Sometimes you can't get a lighter to work. A fire steel is difficult to lose, easy to use and very difficult to get wrong. It lives in the glove box constantly.

TV aerial

16 amp C-form hook-up

Fresh tank filler

ELECTRIC HOOK-UP Electric hook-up – whether it's a 16 amp C-form cable or a complete hook-up kit – means you can connect to campsite electrics and enjoy mains lighting, recharging and running any on-board items like fridges and cookers (some people have them) off the mains.

If you are travelling to Europe, don't forget a two-pin European adaptor.

LEVELLING WEDGES And possibly a spirit level. With a decent pair of levelling wedges you won't have to sleep on a slope. There's art to getting it right and appreciation in a job well done. Your reward for using the spirit level? A great night's sleep.

Note: A glass of water on a flat surface will more than suffice in place of a spirit level.

WATER HOSE If you have an on-board water tank you'll need to be able to fill it up. A length of hose will pay dividends, as many water points don't have them! Even if you have a portable water container it can be a pain to fill if you don't have at least a short length of hose.

UNIVERSAL TAP ATTACHMENTS Carry a set of Hoselock adaptors as well as a universal attachment to fit your hose to any tap.

SHORT LENGTH OF HOSE For swilling out the portaloo. Store separately from your freshwater hose to avoid cross-contamination.

HEAD TORCH Useful for cooking in the dark, walking to the pub, finding the loo or late-night hiking (AKA being lost on a walk). Small enough to pack away tidily in the corner of a cupboard.

MAP Maps tell you everything you need to know about an area. They are wonderful sources of fascination and information. Map reading is a skill and a joy. I would urge everyone to learn how.

SWISS ARMY KNIFE The only tool you'll ever need. Or so they say. Get a good one and you'll be able to do almost anything (almost). Don't bother with the one with two blades and a bottle opener. Go for the big one, with everything. It is a thing to cherish and use, and if it ever goes missing you will be bereft. Know where it is at all times.

EASY-TO-PUT-ON SHOES Slip-ons (such as foam clogs or a pull-on Chelsea boot) are a godsend to the camper as they are easy to put on for middle-of-the-night and early-morning wee trips, are light to carry and are comfortable to wear around the campsite.

DECENT WEATHERPROOF CLOTHES Don't scrimp on the waterproofs. And don't leave them at home. Better to leave them in the van so you'll always have them to hand if the heavens open. Getting cold

and wet is the first step to misery and is difficult to recover from. It can actually be dangerous, too.

LOO PAPER AND FOLDING SPADE The spade is non-essential but could be useful. The loo paper is, of course, vital to a happy trip. And there's nothing like walking across a muddy field with a roll of it early in the morning. Everyone knows where you are off to. No one minds in the least.

Going wild? If you use a spade to bury your doings, make sure you do it at least 200m away from any watercourses and NEVER use wet wipes (they won't break down).

FIRST AID KIT People hurt themselves camping. It's being out of the comfortable zone where nothing exciting ever happens that does it; we relax, let down our guard, enjoy a few glasses of Prosecco and then trips, slips and falls catch us out.

- Plasters
- Scissors
- Bandages
- Gauze and lint for dressing wounds
- Antiseptic cream for cuts and grazes
- Antihistamine cream for bites and stings
- SteriStrips for larger cuts
- Antibacterial hand wash
- Insect repellent
- Sun cream

WASH KIT You might think that you can just lob your usual wash kit into the van and everything will be dandy. It will, of course, but there are a few tips that will make life a lot easier on the road and at a site.

- Take only what you need, otherwise all you're doing is taking a lot of useless wash stuff on a holiday and, ultimately, paying for it in fuel.
- Decant big bottles of shampoo and conditioner into little reusable bottles to take up less space.
- Better still, use solid soaps and shampoos to cut down on waste and make things tidier. Put them in tins to stop them from messing up your wash bag.
- Soap on a rope comes into its own in a camper van. No more dropping the soap. No more mess. No more hassle....

- Men can use shaving soap bars and a shaving brush to save waste and space that might be taken up by aerosol shaving foam.
- Reusable safety razors cut down on space and waste (and will save you oodles of cash).
- Take kit in a wash bag that can be hung from a hook in the cubicle. It'll help you to access it and keep it dry.

Gather your resources

Over the many years I've been travelling, I have found that it is massively useful to gather a camper van library to travel with. It can change for every trip and always remains fluid, depending on the nature of the trip, but the aim is always the same: have vital information to hand. I include in this a list of campsites, addresses of friends to visit, maps, books (like this one), apps to help you along and snippets of information that may or may not be useful.

Of course, since I started travelling they have invented the internet and search engines, which can often render these items useless, but they can come into their own, particularly when you have no signal and the information highway goes offline.

- Apps (that can be used offline)
- Reference books
- Directories of campsites/aires/stopovers
- Maps
- Guide books
- Field guides
- Address book
- Notebook of useful things, clues and snippets
- Membership cards of organisations for discounts/access

Organise your space

Whatever it is you drive, it's a unique space. Your needs are unique, too, which means every van is different, and means different things for different people. How you use that space is entirely up to you.

- Pack the van as a family unit and make sure that everyone knows what goes where.

- Zone your storage. This will enable everyone to find anything at any time as they will know where to look for certain items, even if they aren't in order.
- Make sure that everyone makes the effort to put things back in the right place.
- Organise the van into a 'day mode' and 'night mode' before you go. Everyone will be able to help shift into the right mode and will understand where everything needs to go.
- Get a system going when it comes to making beds and settling down. Make it as easy as possible – no one wants to make a bed when they are falling asleep.
- Make sure the stuff you use most regularly, like levelling wedges, hoses and table legs, are easy to get to. Same with kitchen stuff. Spices that hardly get used but that are still useful to take, for example, go at the back.
- Plastic storage boxes are useful for all kinds of things, especially for stacking, where soft holdalls and bags can be a pain.
- Less is definitely more when it comes to van living.

COOKING KIT

ONE RULE: KEEP IT SIMPLE.

Cooking in a van or motorhome should be about simplicity. The less you take and the more you work within the limits, the happier you'll be. You don't need flashy gadgets. You don't need hundreds of pans. You don't need electrical gizmos.

All you need, really, is fire and a very sharp knife.

Ideally, your ingredients will be bought fresh, and locally too. The idea isn't for you to stock up at a supermarket and take it all with you. That's defeating the object.

Of course it's difficult to give up the convenience of doing your shop all at once in one place. But camping will give you the gift of time, so how about using it to stomp off to the local shops to get your provisions? Swish a stick in the hedgerows, put on a rucksack (no plastic bags please), buy what's local and fresh and give yourself a break from the soulless trolley pushing.

Tips

• Stock up on a few staples before you set off. Then you'll always have enough in your store cupboard for a few emergency dishes.

• Buying local means you get to meet people, find out a little about the place you are visiting, contribute to the local economy and eat fresh. Your shopping makes a positive contribution, small though it may seem.

Kit you need

As we know, cooking can be as simple or as complicated as you want to make it. I prefer it to be fuss-free, with lots of laughter, people poking their noses in, too much wine and kids running everywhere.

So, when it comes to kit, cook with a few well-chosen items instead of gadgetry and gizmos. There's not enough space anyway.

Often, it's a compromise between portability and space when camping. It may also be a matter of cost. But buying cheap or lightweight camping kit won't always help when you are cooking in a van. We aren't yomping over Dartmoor, we are travelling in relative luxury.

So. Here it is. What we travel with.

Pans and pots Think of the size of your cooker rather than the size of your cupboard. If you use tall or small pans on a big ring the heat will go up the sides of the pans and heat up the handles rather than the food. And vice versa. So, choose your pans for the cooker you travel with. Make sure you can get two on the hob at the same time.

Lightweight pans might seem like a good idea but they can burn food more easily than those with heavy bottoms. The heat, even when it's low, can often be too intense. A heavy bottom will make the heat more even.

Chopping boards You don't need colour-coded boards for every eventuality. But I wouldn't travel with just one. Consider a couple of lightweight plastic boards. One for meat, one for veg.

Knives You can't cook without decent knives. And the sharper the better. Don't settle for some rubbish serrated knife from a garage. Bring your best knives, keep them sharp and slice with impunity.

- Large kitchen knife
- Small veg knife
- Bread knife

Veg peeler You could use a knife, but why bother?

Steamer Steaming veg is easier than boiling and the steaming baskets double up as strainers and colanders.

Heavy duty skillet/frying pan Again, it's essential to have a decent frying pan for steaks and breakfasts. It doesn't have to be non-stick, although non-stick is good for pancakes and eggy bread.

BBQ thermometer If you worry about having burgers that are cooked right through, you'll need one of these. Temperatures of more than 75°C will ensure all bugs are killed by the cooking process; 65°C will be enough if you are cooking for at least 10 minutes.

Sieve Not just useful for sieving and draining veg. Can also be used to mash vegetables for soups.

Mixing bowls A couple of lightweight Tupperware bowls are useful for washing, salads, serving and all kinds of other things.

Knives and forks not sporks The spork (a spoon and fork together as one) is good for nothing other than saving space on micro camping adventures. Carry proper cutlery. It's camping, not the dark ages.

Plates and bowls
Melamine won't break or scratch and is light. It also washes more easily than plastic. You can buy melamine picnic sets that are squared off. Might seem obvious but when you are stuck for cupboard space, square plates and bowls can save a fair bit of space.

Cooking sundries

- BBQ tongs
- Metal fish slice
- Spatula/wooden spoons
- Serving spoon
- Ladle
- Whisk
- Masher (useful for soups as well as spuds)
- Washing-up bowl
- Metal or bamboo skewers
- Grater

Marshmallow toasting fork No campfire is complete without toasting marshmallows.

Kitchen essentials Don't forget the basic 'consumables'.

- Cotton dish cloths
- Coconut scourers (can be composted)
- Tea towels
- Eco washing-up liquid
- Fire extinguisher
- Fire blanket
- Kitchen foil

OTHER STUFF IT'S NICE TO HAVE

Paella pan Get one as big as will fit into your cupboard. That might go against all I said above but if you cook over a fire it'll be really useful for cooking a big brekkie for everyone – not to mention a fantastic paella. That's a real treat.

Plancha This is a flat, non-stick hot plate that can go over any heat. It's great for cooking kebabs and breakfasts as well as searing steaks and veg. Also, it doesn't take up too much space.

Herbs and spices

The spice cupboard is a pretty important part of your kitchen equipment. Put together with care and topped up regularly, it'll see you through any number of culinary adventures.

- **Fennel seeds.** Amazing with pork or fish.
- **Smoked paprika.** Hot or sweet, great for flavouring meat and fish.
- **Dried rosemary/basil/ thyme/mint.** Better fresh but handy to have.
- **Herbes de Provence.** A mix that's useful for BBQs and tomato dishes.
- **Turmeric/coriander/ cumin.** For curries
- **Cinnamon.** For sweet and savoury dishes.
- **Nutmeg.** For sweet treats and Dauphinoise.
- **Garam masala.** Another fave for curries.

Condiments and cooking oils

The only thing you really need to carry is some kind of cooking oil.

Decanting oil into lightweight screw-top bottles can help to ensure you won't have spillages if bottles fall over in transit. Small drinks bottles can be useful as they won't break and will seal well. Buy in bulk and decant at home if you have the time.

The rest are useful and don't take up much space. Obviously what condiments and cooking oil you carry is up to you but here's our list:

- Olive oil
- Vegetable oil
- Garlic
- Chillies
- Ginger
- Tomato ketchup
- English mustard powder/ wholegrain
- White wine vinegar
- Soy sauce

Dry staples

Absolutely essential! If you have rice, pasta or noodles then you can always eat, even if it's just pasta and pesto. If you don't want to take a full bag, decant into Tupperware (or old plastic takeaway containers). They are easy to stack and take up less room.

- **Rice/pasta/cous cous**
- **Rice noodles.** Buy them dry from a Chinese supermarket. Place in boiling water and leave for about 10 minutes before using. Easy and quick. And good for you.
- **Risotto rice.** Risotto is so easy and very versatile. Make it with just about anything for a super-filling meal.
- **Linguine.** Flat spaghetti; easy and quick, good with anything.
- **Chorizo.** Lasts for ages.
- **Lentils.** Last for a while, great for bulking up soups and stews.
- **White flour.** Useful for making pitas and thickening Coq au Van.
- **Tins of tomatoes, coconut milk, chickpeas.**

COOKING METHODS AND HEAT SOURCES

Equipment

INDUCTION HOB More common in our homes than in vans, induction hobs use electric induction to create instant heat. Massively versatile and only made possible by lithium-ion batteries, which give 220V  and can be charged quickly using solar or a split relay charge. Does away with the need for fuel tanks or bottles. Requires lots of power.

DIESEL BURNER Another cooking device that does away with the need for separate fuel as it runs off the diesel tank. Not as controllable as induction but can produce a good heat. The burner exhausts to the outside of the van. Requires expert installation.

TRIPOD Using a tripod with a hanging something underneath it is a truly time-honoured way of cooking. A pot, suspended over a fire, fully adjustable and hugely versatile.

KOTLICH The *kotlich* is a traditional Hungarian enamelled pot and tripod kit that's great for cooking stews but also comes with a suspended grill. The firepit has legs so it's off the ground. **kotlichcooking.co.uk**

DUTCH OVEN Cast-iron Dutch ovens are suitable for hanging from tripods and will also stand in a fire (they have little feet). The lid on a decent Dutch oven should also have a lip so you can shovel embers on top of it without them falling in the food. Good for making damper bread.

CADAC CARRI CHEF
The Cadac is a versatile piece of cooking kit that comes from South Africa. It's basically a single burner that runs straight from a gas canister (or BBQ gas point) with lots of interchangeable bits and pieces like a griddle, grill plate and the brilliant and very useful Skottel, a dish-shaped hot plate that's like a flattened wok.

The Cadac can also be used as a BBQ in areas where you can't have fires.

PORTABLE CAMP STOVE Portable worktop stoves are cheap and produce a good heat but use disposable canisters that aren't that cheap to buy. Handy, but wasteful.

GHILLIE KETTLE/KELLY KETTLE

These little stoves are wonderful if you have the space and are looking to make boiling water in a hurry. They use virtually any dry fuel and very little of it, and will boil water in just a few minutes. You can also cook on them if you need to with a range of accessories that turn the base into a basic cooker.

ROCKET STOVE

Rocket stoves work on the same principle as Kelly (or Ghillie) Kettles. They use little fuel but burn it with lots of oxygen to make a fierce flame that burns bright and hot for as long as it gets fed. They squeeze a lot of heat out of a few twigs and therefore are particularly useful if there isn't much fuel in the way of dry logs to be had.

COBB

The Cobb is a miracle, so they say. It's compact and neat, and packs down small enough for most camping trips. It'll also do all kinds of great stuff, such as the legendary beer can chicken, which is what everyone did on it when they first came out. As time has gone on they have become more and more versatile and now come in a gas version as well as the original cobblestone version.

YOUR IN-VAN STOVE

If you have a standard one it might have two rings and a grill. Otherwise, you might just have two rings, or even just one. Just make sure you get pans that fit. There is little that is more frustrating that trying to boil a kettle and cook a breakfast at the same time when the pans are too big and will not fit on the stove at the same time.

Some motorhomes have induction hobs or electric plates that can only be used when plugged into a site.

Fuel for cooking (and heating)

Aside from wood for a fire and BBQ briquettes or Cobb cobblestones, there are a number of ways of generating heat for cooking.

Electricity Lithium-ion batteries make it possible to have microwaves and induction hobs in vans. Previously impossible solutions are now available to all.

Your diesel tank See page 66 for information on a diesel burner. Useful and avoids the need for gas tanks or bottles.

Isobutane/butane This is the gas that comes in your standard blue Campingaz containers. It is available universally throughout Europe, burns well, provides a good heat and produces an easily adjustable flame.

However, it doesn't burn well at temperatures below 4°C and stops vaporising at −1°C, so is not good for cold weather camping.

Propane/LPG Propane gas or LPG is often the option for motorhomes. It usually comes in red containers or grey and green for patio gas. Some motorhomes have on-board tanks that can be refilled at petrol stations. Propane won't stop vaporising until around −27°C so it's the only option in colder climes.

Gas and BBQ safety

When cooking in a camper van or motorhome it's important to ensure that you use gas safely and understand the risks of cooking with BBQs.

- Do not cook in your van unless you have adequate ventilation. Keep a vent, all the windows or the door open.
- Make sure you turn your gas supply off at the cylinder (regulator) before you travel.
- If you suspect a leak, open all doors and windows, turn off the supply and get the help of an expert.
- If you suspect a flexible pipe or joint is leaking, use a washing-up liquid and water solution on it. Gas will bubble through it.
- Get your gas equipment checked regularly by a qualified gas fitter.
- Change rubber gas hoses regularly for use with BBQs and stoves.
- Change cylinders in the open air, or at least with the doors to the camper or motorhome wide open.
- If you have vents in the compartment where your gas is stored, make sure they are unobstructed. If you don't have vents, get some fitted by an expert.
- Carry a fire extinguisher on board. Keep it nearby when cooking or using BBQs.
- Do not attempt to refill gas canisters unless they are designed for that purpose.
- Don't use disposable BBQs in an enclosed space. NEVER light them in a van or motorhome. They give off lots of deadly CO fumes

Alternative kitchens

THE COOKING POD The idea of a removable pod that can be taken out of a Transporter is nothing new, but it has come into its own in recent times as a cheap alternative to a full conversion. Lots of camper companies are now making pods that can be removed when not in use.

Modular kitchens can be really useful as they can turn an ordinary van into a camper easily, making the vehicle more versatile than ever and even allowing you to lift them out to use in a tent or awning.

- Cambee's lift-out camper kitchen, the Picnic Pod (used in their 'Go' conversion) is like a glorified buddy box with extra bits, a removable stove and space to stash the cutlery and bits and pieces. **www.cambee.co.uk**
- Slidepods are designed to fit under the rear seat of a VW Kombi or Beach but can be made for just about any day van. They slide out on rails and have fresh and waste tanks, cooker and a sink. **www.slidepods.co.uk**
- Vangear make all kinds of combination pods for day vans that are designed to fit on to floor rails. **www.vangear.co.uk**
- Auto Campers make an entirely unique modular system that includes beds and kitchens. **www.auto-campers.co.uk**

Open fires

Having a fire is an essential part of camping. A real fire takes us back, on a primal level, to days when staring at the embers was a critical part of survival.

Today, though, we exist in a time when there are rules about lighting fires. Some campsites do allow fires but these are few and far between. Often, in Europe, where fire danger poses a real risk to dry forest and habitats, BBQs are banned in all but the most controlled places.

www.campfiresburning.org, **www.pitchup.com** and **www. coolcamping.com** all have lists of sites in the UK where campfires are allowed.

FIRE PITS There are times when fire pits may be allowed but lighting a fire on the ground is not. This is where a Roadii or kotlich or some other type of fire pit that won't burn grass is going to come in useful.

Top fire-lighting tips

As with many things, preparation is everything. Make sure you have enough tinder, kindling and fuel that it is dry and that you have enough matches and/or a lighter that works. Also make sure you have a method of controlling your fire if it were to get out of hand. A fire blanket, extinguisher or, at the very least, a bucket of water will do it.

Don't be tempted to pour petrol, WD40, oil or any flammable substance on your fire to encourage it.

- **Tinder** is what you use to start the fire; it could be rolled-up newspaper, firelighters (no it's not cheating), dry grass or cotton wool.
- **Kindling** is the smaller twigs and finely chopped wood that is used to get the fire going once the tinder is lit.
- **Big kindling** is useful as a halfway house for logs if you are using them complete.
- **Chopping logs** in half makes them easier to light.
- **Digging a fire pit** and then encircling it with rocks will create a good pit in which to light your fire. It will also help to contain it should it get out of control.

- **DO NOT** light your fire anywhere near flammable items such as dry grass, fences, trees or peaty soil.
- **Keep a bucket of water** handy at all times in case your fire gets out of hand.
- **If you are thinking of lighting a fire on grass**, don't, as it will kill it. If you must, at least dig out a sod of turf, light the fire in the hole and replace the sod afterwards, once the fire is fully out.
- **Beware of lighting fires on stones** or flint, which may chip and explode with heat.
- **Put the tinder at the bottom**, place a few bits of light kindling on top and light the tinder. Add kindling as it catches either in a square shape, narrowing as it piles up, or in a pyramid shape, and make sure there is adequate airflow. Don't add too much or you may smother the flames.
- **NEVER LEAVE YOUR FIRE** to burn out unattended. If you have to depart, make sure it is put out completely and that the environment is put back exactly as it was. DO NOT leave mess, nails from old wood or litter.

COOLING

Keeping food cool is essential for food safety. 'At risk' foods, such as dairy, meat, fish and pastry, should always be kept at a temperature of less than 8°C. Any toxins or pathogens in food are inactive below 8°C. Leave 'at risk' foods (poultry, seafood and pork) above 8°C for any long period and you could risk your health. Your cool box and fridge are vital pieces of equipment.

Camping fridges

There are three different cooling methods for fridges (described opposite) and three ways a fridge can be powered: by 12V from the battery or solar, by gas or by 240V from a mains hook-up.

What's in your camper will determine the way you use it, as some types of fridges can kill leisure batteries. This will also help to determine the type you might choose when kitting out a van or motorhome.

ABSORPTION FRIDGES

This is the method that many camper van fridges work on. It relies on a concentrated ammonia solution being heated by a boiler, giving off a vapour that is then condensed and evaporated. The process draws heat out of the storage container (fridge), so cooling it.

Advantages	Disadvantages
• Can be run on LPG or butane gas • Can be run on 12V or 240V mains • Silent in operation • Cheaper than compressor fridges • Available in a range of 'standard' camper van sizes	• Can only be run on 12V for short periods or when the vehicle is moving (and therefore charging the leisure battery) • Will drain a leisure battery (and kill it) in a matter of hours • Must be vented externally to allow dangerous gas fumes from the boiler to escape

Information for this section very kindly supplied by O'Briens Camping.
www.obrienscamping.co.uk

COMPRESSOR FRIDGES

Compressor fridges work by pushing a coolant, either as a gas or liquid, through a series of pipes. The coolant pulls warmth out of the cooling compartment then gives it out again as pipes narrow at the back of the fridge.

Advantages	Disadvantages
• More efficient cooling, with the possibility of ice boxes • Can be run on solar power • Easier to install • No need for external ventilation, as there are no fumes • Pull much less battery power than an absorption fridge	• Can be noisy • More expensive than absorption fridges

PORTABLE THERMOELECTRIC COOLERS

Thermoelectric cooling relies on electricity to power elements that give off heat and cooling energy. They are then enhanced by heat exchangers and air fans to drop the temperature of a cool box to below the ambient temperature.

Some cool boxes can be used with gas as well as 12V and 240V, so combining absorption and compression features. These cannot be used inside a camper on gas as they will not be sufficiently vented.

Advantages	*Disadvantages*
● Portable and can be run on 12V or 240V ● Can be light and easy to carry ● Low-cost solution	● Only cool to around 30°C below ambient temperature. In very hot climates this may not be sufficient ● Cannot be used on gas power inside

COOL BOXES

For campers without fridges, cool boxes are the next best thing. Depending on the amount of insulation they contain, the ambient outside temperature and how often they are opened and closed, a cool box can remain cool for up to 24 hours or so.

Cool boxes will need to be topped up with cooler packs to remain cool. Some campsites will freeze them down for you.

Chillin' tips

● **Some campsites have freezers** where you can put your freezer packs overnight. Mark them as yours with indelible pen.

● **If your campsite doesn't have** a freezer, you could try burying them in the freezer department of the local supermarket and then going back for them later.

● **If you are short of space,** freeze bottles of water (or milk) before you go and place them in the fridge or cool box. They will help to bring down the temperature more quickly, so putting less demand on the fridge. If you use milk it'll help it to keep longer.

Top tips for camper van cooking

1 Remember that eating local, seasonal food means it's fresh and has fewer food miles. Finding local food can lead to interesting food adventures.

2 Always ensure you have at least one back-up plan.

3 Keep it simple: cook with good ingredients, as few pots and pans as possible and without the need for gadgetry.

4 Decant olive oil, cooking oil, vinegars and similar into clean plastic, screw-cap bottles to save weight and for refilling.

5 Put butter in jam jars to stop it melting or getting messy.

6 Decant flour, pasta and nuts etc into Tupperware pots for ease of storage and for refilling at waste-free shops.

7 Invest in a set of melamine plates. They are light and won't break like china, burn like tin plates or break down like plastic.

8 Make sure you take basics you can't get anywhere but home: tea bags...Marmite... Worcestershire Sauce.

9 Invest in a small, portable gas BBQ if you love to BBQ. You'll still be able to use it at campsites where open fires are banned.

10 Check you have enough gas before you start a stew.

11 Don't forget the marshmallows if you're travelling with kids. It's the rules!

WHERE TO SPEND THE NIGHT

Now we are getting down to it! This is what it's all about. Sleeping is the whole point of the camper van or motorhome experience. Without it, the camper van would just be...well...a van.

Overnighting is the raison d'être of this cult we call camper van.

Of course everyone is different and everyone has different needs, wants and desires. But at the heart of it all is the idea of freedom, of waking somewhere new, of the endless possibilities given to you by a new day, of escaping to somewhere other than humdrum, of exploration and finding new experiences, places and things, and of appreciating the outdoors.

If you are new to camper vanning or motorhoming then I would like to spend the next 20 or so pages going through some of the options available to you. I think it's important to know what's open to you so you can make your own choices about what you aspire to, feel comfortable with or simply like the sound of.

I will go through each option and explain the pros and cons. I hope it won't offend you if I point out some of the basic stuff, especially if you already camp regularly, but it's important to get it right. Staying in the wrong kind of place can make or break a trip.

Of course the best thing about your motorhome or camper van is that you can up sticks and move on to somewhere better if you don't like it. The secret though, is to know what you like and head there first.

And that's what this section is all about.

Campsites

Campsites come in all shapes and sizes: big, small, quirky, wild, manicured, regimented, noisy, quiet, boring, whatever. Every one of them is different. However, we can generally class them in types so at least you know what to expect. Sort of.

TYPES OF CAMPSITES

Holiday/touring parks

These are the giants of the leisure industry. Usually owned by large companies or groups, like Hoseasons, Parkdean or Haven, they often have a mix of camping, touring (pitches for caravans and motorhomes) and chalets (mobile homes).

A lot of holiday parks also include family activities and attractions, with some of the larger parks having pools, bars, restaurants, a golf course, amusements, whatever. You may find that camping pitches are limited. In any case, expect to be among families, kids and the whole of humanity in its many forms and all of its wondrous beauty.

PROS ▸ Lots for everyone to do. Fun for the kids.

CONS ▸ Not everyone likes big sites with lots of chalets and mobile homes.

Pop-up summer sites

Some campsites pop up in the summertime only, so taking advantage of the 28-day rule (in the UK) that allows campsites to have a temporary licence. These can often be just for camper vans and motorhomes as they have no real facilities, or they share facilities with a shop, bar or cafe. Some people call them aires.

PROS ▸ It's normally all about the location, so they can be situated in great places.

CONS ▸ In my experience, there's few facilities other than loos and water, if that.

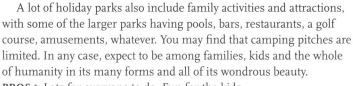

Small/independent sites Lots of campers like to turn their backs on the kind of 'civilised' camping and go for a more natural camping experience. This may be a working farm or someone fulfilling their dream of owning a nice campsite. Often gems, sometimes basic and occasionally in spectacular locations.

When you want to see countryside or beach out of your camper van window rather than a sea of mobile homes and static caravans, the small site is the way to go. This is camping as it should be (if you ask me), the way I remember it from when I was a boy, except the shower block and facilities have been upgraded.

These are the kind of sites that people revere and talk about on forums. If you find a good one, keep it to yourself. It may not have a website or online booking. You may be required just to turn up.

See **www.pitchup.com**, **www.campsited.com**, **www.coolcamping.com** or **www.campsites.co.uk** for the best UK and European selection.

PROS ▶ Camping how it should be. In a field, away from the trappings.
CONS ▶ You might not get wi-fi.

Club sites There are two camping and caravanning clubs in the UK. The Camping and Caravanning Club (C&CC) is the oldest. It began life in 1901 as the Association of Cycle Campers and today welcomes campers, caravans, camper vans and motorhomes. They offer insurance, online booking, a network of sites and help and advice, plus discounts.

The advantage of staying on club sites is that the experience is often very similar from site to site. You are guaranteed a good washroom experience, checking in is generally on the same terms and the approach is similar. They also have a 6m rule, which guarantees distance between you and your neighbour. Sometimes they can be a little too regimented, with rules for how you pitch.

PROS ▶ Well-organised sites, with wardens, good-quality showers and often extra facilities. Good washrooms. Great for wash and brush-up days with standard experiences. Good locations.

CONS ▶ Can be a little regimented and may feel corporate. You may feel surrounded by white boxes.

Certificated Locations (Caravan and Motorhome Club) and Certificated Sites (Camping and Caravanning Club)

These are small, privately run sites that are allowed to offer pitches for no more than five units (or 10 tents if a C&CC CS). There are thousands of them all over the UK. Often on farms or run as a side business. You must be a member of the club to stay, which makes it all the more worthwhile joining. It is often advisable to book in advance (usually just call ahead). These sites are often out of the way, in interesting places where big sites wouldn't be allowed. For more see **www.caravanclub.co.uk** and **www.campingandcaravanclub.co.uk**

PROS ▶ Great locations on private land, often secluded and quiet with just a few other campers.

CONS ▶ Fewer facilities than bigger sites. Directories will show what facilities are available. May need to have your own loo.

Adults only So you don't like kids? That's OK. Other people don't like them either. And it may be best if you all stick together so you can find a little peace and quiet on your just-for-grown-ups campsite. It's a shame that some sites prefer not to hear the joyous laughter of kids being healthy, outdoor children but that's the way it is.

PROS ▶ If you are allergic to kids then this is your kind of camping.

CONS ▶ If you have kids, you can't go.

Naturist clubs and sites There is something beautiful about going wild when you are going wild. I am not a naturist but I see nothing wrong with stripping off and baring all. If your camping experiences include wanting to let the sun see the whole of you, then there are lots of options, with more in Europe than in the UK (perhaps for obvious reasons).

Alan Rogers, provider of guidebooks and camping directories, has a list of naturist campsites all over Europe: **www.alanrogers.com**

PROS ▶ If you want to be among naked people there's no better way to camp.

CONS ▶ Are there any? For naturists, perfect. Weather dependent.

Campsite alternatives

AIRES AND OVERNIGHTS 'Aires' is the common (UK) name for *'aires de camping car'* (motorhome area). These are overnight parking places that are specifically designated for motorhomes and camper vans. The system is prevalent in France, although it is spreading throughout Europe, with guides now available for France, Belgium, Germany, Italy, Spain, Portugal, Holland and Luxembourg from **www.vicariousbooks.co.uk**.

The idea is that local councils (or private individuals) provide an overnight stop for self-contained motorhomes. Tents and caravans are not allowed, neither is putting out tables and chairs or awnings. Most aires have fresh water and facilities for emptying waste water and toilet tanks – these are known as service points. Some have electricity. Some charge for the privilege and others don't. Some provide showers and toilets, others just the basics – a parking place and somewhere to empty the Porta Potti. Local police will often make daily rounds and take number plates to ensure no one abuses the system.

I understand why the French have aires. They offer a neat solution to some problems. With designated places, they can police who stays overnight and control illegal camping on the roadside or at beauty spots (they are using a similar technique in the Scottish Islands). They can also control a little of the flow of traffic through busy summer resorts by signposting the aires via quiet routes or by placing them on the edge of town. It works. The system also works to attract people to a town and gives them a reason to visit. If there is a cheap place to stay, people will come and spend money in the town.

I wish there were more in the UK and Ireland (more are popping up in Ireland all the time) and applaud independently minded councils who set them up (Torridge District Council, well done!) because they attract NEW audiences, do not detract from local tourism businesses and bring new revenue.

BRITSTOPS Britstops is the British version of the highly popular France Passion scheme that puts producers, cafes, restaurants and bars in touch with motorhomers. The hosts offer a free night (and often no facilities) on their land in exchange for a simple 'hello'. There is no obligation to buy anything although if you stay in a pub car park you know where you'll end up.

The guide costs £28 or so and gives you a year's worth of 'invitations' to stay on more than 1,000 sites all across the UK and Ireland. These vary but are mostly pubs. The guide includes details of a number of spaces, whether you have to call ahead and if there are any facilities.

There is no charge for staying, only the obligation that you will say 'hello' and 'goodbye' as you leave. To take advantage of the scheme you must be self-contained and own the current guide, available from **www.britstops.com**.

There are similar schemes in Italy and Spain. Buy the guides, including France Passion, from **www.vicariousbooks.co.uk**.

Wild or free camping

This is camping off-grid, away from campsites or alternatives, freely, in the wild. It's the Shangri-La of the camping world and lots of camper van and motorhome owners aspire to it.

In recent times there has been much made of wild camping, caused by those who choose to abuse the right. During the summer of 2020, places that are usually open to wild camping (in tents primarily) have shut down as a result of antisocial behaviour and the sheer numbers of people wanting to get out and into the countryside.

The idea is great, in practice it may not be.

I love 'free' or 'off-site' camping. I've done it regularly, ever since I started sleeping in vans. Sometimes, in winter, it was a necessity. I slept in boatyards, on quaysides, among dunes and in pub car parks just to be able to go for an early surf. And it was brilliant fun. I still do it now.

But the fact remains that wild camping is illegal in England and Wales.

The Caravan Sites and Control of Development Act 1960* makes it a civil offence to pitch your tent or park your camper without permission on someone else's land or to operate a caravan site or campsite without a licence. There are exceptions (for clubs and societies and for licensed gatherings) but on the whole the Act means that you are causing an offence by camping on unlicensed sites without permission.

Landowners, too, are restricted by the amount of time that they can allow anyone to camp on their land, even with permission. They may allow one caravan, motorhome or camper van to stay overnight, for no more than two nights in succession and for no more than 28 days in any 12-month period. However, wild camping is a civil offence, which means that it is a matter for the courts, not the police. You make your own choices there but it is as well to remember that parking up on the hard shoulder or in a lay-by (that is a part of the public highway) means

* You can read the Act in full at this website: www.legislation.gov.uk/ukpga/Eliz2/8-9/62

that the police do have the power to move you on, if they consider you are causing an obstruction. Although in my experience a policeman in a good mood would rather see you snatch a few hours' kip than drive tired.

At the time of writing, trespass (wild camping on other's land without permission) is a civil offence but the government is making moves to make it illegal, which means the police will have the power to remove and arrest you if a complaint is made against you.

At the side of the road isn't always OK. How many times have you found a beautiful parking spot – an esplanade or lay-by or car park – only to find you can't stay for the night because of the 'no overnight parking' signs? It's infuriating. But is it legally enforceable?

There seems to be plenty of stuff on this, and everywhere is different, but the crux of the matter is that if you are not causing an obstruction and are parked legally, it may not be enforceable. However, as is the case in parts of Scotland, if there is evidence of the local by-law or traffic regulation order on the sign, then it may be. Traffic regulation orders are legal documents that restrict or prohibit use of the highway network. They can be concerned with parking and prohibition of certain types of vehicles and may be enforceable with fines.

This may be the case when councils decide to ban overnighting in camper vans at hotspots, car parks and in places where residents have complained about antisocial behaviour and mess (or just don't like motorhomes) or there have been historic problems with narrow streets, overcrowding or disrespectful overnighting. It may also be that some councils don't want you staying in their towns and spending money in their shops. The best thing to do? Go somewhere else!

WILD CAMPING IN NATIONAL PARKS There are some areas in national parks where it is legal to wild camp. However, that's for the tented folk. If you want to, you risk being moved on by the rangers. In the summer of 2020, some national parks banned wild camping because of the number of people doing it and leaving litter behind.

WILD CAMPING IN SCOTLAND The Promised Land!!!! Or is it? The Land Reform Act makes wild camping legal on public access land. It is a great and truly liberating thing that means Scotland is viewed as the Promised Land of wild camping by wannabe wild campers all over the UK. But it isn't without its problems.

Wild camping: the rules

This is simple. Please follow these rules:

● Leave it nicer than it was when you arrived. Take your litter home. If you can, pick up others' litter and take it home too. It will create a good impression of you.

● Do not empty tanks of any type anywhere you are not authorised. Take it with you until you are able to dispose of it properly.

● If you can, get permission from the landowner.

● Do not light fires or BBQs unless you know it is approved by the landowner.

● Arrive late and leave early.

● Don't set up camp, hang out washing or get out all your tables and chairs and windbreaks, etc. Others might see it as preparing to stay a long time.

● Don't pitch up near houses or blocking anyone's views.

● Be prepared to defend your right to wild camp by ensuring others don't break the rules either.

● Don't play loud music or act in an unsociable way.

● If you are asked to move on, do it with a smile.

The Land Reform Act makes no mention of motorhomes or camper vans and it is an assumption that wild camping is legal. The Scottish Outdoor Access Code also makes no mention of wild camping in vehicles.

If there was one recurring story in the motorhome world in 2020 it was that wild campers – and we get lumped in with that lot – have been making a big mess in Scotland. This is due to overcrowding and lack of care. What will happen – as has happened in Loch Lomond and the Trossachs National Park – is that hotspots get zoned and wild camping will require a permit. The best way to avoid this is simply to follow the wild camping rules.

WILD CAMPING IN EUROPE In my experience, wild camping is easier in Spain and France than in the UK, with Spain marginally ahead in terms of ease. France's aire system takes care of a lot of the problems they have had with wild camping (mess and disrespect) in organised areas. But there are places where wild camping is tolerated. In some areas, such as the Côte d'Azur, local by-laws have made it virtually impossible to stay in beachside car parks or in lay-bys. Don't be surprised if you get the knock in the night.

In Spain, I have free camped all along the north coast without any problems. It is tolerated at many spots and has become a part of life at some surf destinations – even though it may not be strictly legal. There are laws that prohibit camping within 200m of the beach and in other places, like near military zones, national parks and plenty of other places. Some of the regions ban wild camping altogether while others allow it as long as there are no more than three units, fewer than 10 people and you stay no more than three days. Whatever the rules and how you interpret them, respect is always the order of the day.

In Scandinavian countries, including Norway and Sweden, there are certain rights of the individual to roam and have access to land. In fact, as a nation with rights of access and the right to commune with nature embedded in its culture and law, Norway has some of the most liberal access laws of any country. However, it also comes with rules, such as not camping within 150m of a house or on uncultivated lands, in young forest or where it may cause environmental damage.

Final tip: Leave it nicer.

Places to stay en route

Got a long way to go? Then you'd better plan for a stop along the way. There are some options open to you, however each one comes with a caveat. Of course it does. Nothing is ever simple.

THE FIRST RULE OF THE HALFWAY HOUSE You may get asked to move on, wherever you stay without express permission, so the last thing to do is have a glass of wine with supper. If the police come knocking and don't like the smell of you, you could end up spending the rest of the night in gaol, or jail, or worse.

THE SECOND RULE OF THE HALFWAY HOUSE If you stay in a public place then it will either be the police or the local authority who has the responsibility for that space. They have different powers, but ultimately they can move you on, wherever you are.

TYPES OF PLACES TO STAY EN ROUTE

Car parks and motorway services Every car park is different and will have different rules. Some motorway services will slap a ticket on you if you don't buy a ticket for time over two hours (supermarkets can do this too). In the UK, these 'fines' aren't issued by the police or local councils and are usually just 'invoices'.

Truck stops Looking for a good brekkie? This is the place to stop. Just be careful, park away from traffic, don't block anyone in and steer clear of the arm wrestling contest.

Oh, and securely lock your doors and windows and keep everything out of sight.

Stealth camping Some campers don't look like campers. That enables them to go under the radar of the authorities and stay in places other campers wouldn't even consider. It's at your own risk. But the same rules apply: if you get moved on, go. If you have a drink, be prepared for the consequences.

Planning overnights

Not everyone likes to plan their trip down to the tiniest detail, but it can help to have a rough idea of where you might stay from one night to the next. If you are touring it can become a job in itself working out where to stay, with lots of resources needed to plan ahead, even if it's only an hour ahead.

Some tips for advance overnight planning:

• At the very least, get your first night sorted in advance, at a campsite where you can spend a little time getting used to living in your van again. Get there before dark and leave as late as possible to not be in a rush.

• Use the searchforsites app, or similar apps, to find options near you (see page 125).

• If you are planning on wild camping, make sure you know where you will be able to fill up and empty so you aren't tempted to empty waste on the fly. This is NOT good. Find campsite alternatives that you could head to when you need that wash and brush-up.

• Look at the options for aires or motorhome stopovers so you have somewhere to go in case you get moved on or can't find anywhere else suitable.

• Plan on taking a couple of days 'off' every week or so to give you a chance to stop and rest. If you are continually on the move, it can be tiring packing up day after day. Having a morning when you can leave the bed out can be a tonic!

• Remember that you can always move if you don't like a site.

BEDS, FOAM AND MATTRESSES

This is what it's all about: what you sleep on. Often, you won't have much of a choice if you are buying second hand but if you are choosing a new van, converting a van or changing things around, it's an important consideration. After all, you'll spend about eight hours a day in it, so the bed needs to be good.

How big is your bed?

Rock and roll beds

A rock and roll bed is a seat that turns into a bed. There are lots of different types to go for, with lots of options, ranging from fully crash tested, 100 per cent compliant, touch-of-a-button British-made steel constructions, to wood and hinges kits that look decidedly un-crash ready.

Rock and roll beds for standard-sized camper vans come in two sizes: full width and three-quarter width.

FULL-WIDTH BEDS Full-width beds are fantastic for families that have children who like to creep in with mum and dad in the night. They are great for the whole family to lay about in and even better if you like a lot of space to sleep in.

The drawback with a full-width bed is that space is limited for other stuff, like cupboards, cookers and sinks. It means all your stuff is going to be up front, out of the way of the bed as it swings forwards. The bonus is that there's more room in the back. Having travelled extensively in a T2 with a full-width bed I can safely say it's great. You just gotta be tidy.

THREE-QUARTER WIDTH BEDS The three-quarter width bed is something of a standard with smaller camper vans. This is because it allows for a full set of units to be installed along one side of the van, so allowing plenty of worktop space and under-cupboard space for clothes, kit, cooking gear and fridges. Three-quarter width beds make it a lot easier to be tidy by using wardrobes and cupboards for clothes and suchlike, but the bed space is more limited. It also means that when not being used as a camper – as a day-to-day vehicle – they aren't quite so versatile. And by that I mean less space for carrying wardrobes.

ROCK AND ROLL COMPLIANCE Rock and roll. It was never supposed to be governed by rules, compliance and legislation. But sadly it is, especially if it's a rock and roll bed.

Rock and roll beds are not only an important part of the camping set-up of many smaller campers but they're also a vital part of the seating arrangements. That means they have two jobs to do: sleeping and seating.

The EU now dictates that new motor caravans (camper vans) need to be type approved, which includes testing and assessment against EU standards for seat belts, anchorage points for the seat belts and the strength of seats and their mountings.

However, when it comes to converting existing vans with rock and roll beds and converting them into motor caravans, the seats are not subject to the same demands, although they are subject to road vehicles' regulations demanding similar standards for seat belts and anchorage points, but not of seat mounting strength. What this says is: 'a motor vehicle, and all its parts and accessories; the number of passengers carried, and the manner in which any passengers are carried in or on a vehicle; and the weight, distribution, packing and adjustment of the load of a vehicle, to be at all times such that no danger is caused, or is likely to be caused, to any person in or on a vehicle or on a road' ('Carriage of Passengers in a Horsebox', UK Department for Transport).

Pull and crash tests Some rock and roll beds are subject to testing. This is often a 'pull test', whereby the seat is pulled by a mechanism that exerts similar forces on the seat as would happen if a vehicle were to stop very suddenly (crash). Depending on the number of passengers a seat is designed to carry, rock and roll beds get pull tested for 3 (one person), 7 (two people) or 11 tonnes (three people). This is a test of the strength of the seat and seat belts, not necessarily of the loading points of the seat (where it fixes to the chassis).

Some manufacturers also send their bed frames off for 'in-vehicle' crash testing, which will actually test the strength of the mountings as well as the seat itself. Often, these manufacturers will add extra strengthening to the chassis in order to be able to cope with high loads.

Other manufacturers will also test their seats with 'sled tests', whereby the seats are tested on sleds that move backwards and forwards, so creating a more 'realistic' scenario.

Putting safety first There are lots of rock and roll beds on the market. Some are pull tested, some in-vehicle tested, few sled tested. Many are compliant. Only you can make big decisions about the integrity and safety of the products you put in your van. However, if it were me making those decisions, I would go for the most rigorously tested, approved design I could afford. It's precious cargo aboard.

Reputable makes include: Reimo, Titan and Rib Altair.

Note: In the UK there can be differing restrictions on seats in vehicles in M or N classes, depending on the DVLA category.

Fixed bed campers

This is the height of luxury: a bed that stays made all day long so you can simply crawl into it at night. No putting on sheets or zipping up sleeping bags or moving boxes. No putting everything in the front seats. No putting the seat up to drive away in the morning even. What's more, you get acres of space underneath for storage. And, on top of it all, you get to sleep on a real mattress, with springs and memory foam and all that malarkey.

The bad news? This kind of luxury is only for the bigger vans and motorhomes where it's not that important to make best use of every single inch of space. Often, Boxer-sized vans will only sleep two with a fixed bed.

In some motorhomes, however, where the fixed bed is above the cab, this can significantly add to the available living space – and makes a good spot for storing stuff during the day (although if you do that, you'll still have to clear it all up to get into bed). And it's not so easy getting up the ladder after a couple of vino plonkos. Better to make it the kids' domain and let them use it.

Some Hymer motorhomes from the 1980s have beds that lower down over the cab at night. This is also useful, as you can leave the sheet and duvet on to stow – so saving time later and making more of the living space.

Drop-down beds

These are becoming more and more popular in motorhomes as a way of stashing a bed out of the way during the day (and keeping it made), without taking up the space of the fixed bed. The idea here is that the bed winches into the ceiling during the day. They do reduce headroom and can add to the cost but are surprisingly useful, often allowing a two berth-sized van to sleep four.

Transverse beds

These are beds that run across the width of a van or motorhome. They require a vehicle to be at least 6ft 2" (1.9m) wide so they fit properly (it's usually no problem in a motorhome) and can allow a lot more to be fitted into a shorter vehicle. Fiat Ducato and Peugeot Boxers are well suited for transverse beds as they are wide enough, whereas VW Crafters and Mercedes Sprinters are narrower and tend to taper towards the roof, making transverse beds too short. However, there are window pods available that extend the width of the van by putting 'bubbles' into the rear panels. They are particularly suited to vans that have garages below a transverse bed as they tend to sit too high for seating.

Make up beds

These are beds that have to be constructed every night and disassembled every morning as they are made from various bits and pieces, such as a table top or special sections that live in the cupboards during the day. They are typical of motorhomes and larger campers where seating can be arranged into day and night modes, or changed around for 'lounge' or driving positions. The back of the seat cushions double up as bed cushions that are used for the base of the day seat, and so on.

It's all a part of what it means to be in a camper van. Unless you have a fixed bed or drop-down bed you will, at some point, face the making of the bed. In the darkness or the half-light you'll forget where everything is supposed to go, get it all wrong and wake up in a pile of cushions.

TIPS FOR MAKING THE BED

- If your cushions have knee supports, turn them around and put them under your head. This is much better than having them under your bum in the middle of the night.
- Draw a map of your bed and the way it is supposed to be. Tape it to the inside of one of your cupboards.

A guide to bedding foam

If you are home converting or choosing new foam it's worth noting that foam isn't just foam. Here's a quick run through:

The first thing to remember is that comfort is relative.

The second thing you need to remember is to think about what your cushions are to be used for predominantly. Are they to be used as seating or are they to be used as bedding?

UNDERSTANDING FOAM GRADES Foam is graded by foam type, density, hardness and volume.

On your quest for a decent night's sleep you may come across foam grades such as 3in V38/200 or the heady combination of a classic 4in R40/180. You lucky people. Let's explain...

Type Foam type is the basic name for any particular type of foam.

- V is for foam that is 'heavy domestic and contract quality'. A quality foam that is best suited for sitting and seat cushions and will last well. Generally 30 per cent cheaper than Reflex (below) and better suited to sitting than sleeping.
- R is for Reflex, a brand name. This is a very high-quality latex foam that will retain its properties over time. The best quality for sleeping.
- CMHR is for 'Combustion Modified High Resilience Foam' that includes a lot of melamine for flame retardancy. It tends to powder over time and can retain moisture, so this type is not recommended for camper vans.
- RECON is reconditioned foam. It is made up from all the off-cuts. It is generally poor wearing, very heavy and not much use to anyone, although it is cheap. Avoid.

Density Foam density is the weight of the foam in kilograms per cubic metre. The higher the number, the higher the density. A high-density foam will last longer and be of better quality. Expect to see density of around 38–40 for a decent foam.

Hardness Hardness is measured in Newtons. It's all about the science here, so I shall skip that and say to the layman, the hardness is all about the comfort. Typical foams for campers come in at anywhere between 135–200 Newtons, depending on the comfort required.

The rule for choosing foam based on hardness:

- If you're sitting more than sleeping, use a high-density V grade foam. If it's less firm, go for extra thickness. V40/200 at 3in is a good bet for camper van cushions.
- If you're sleeping more than sitting, use a thicker but less firm Reflex foam. Try something like a R38/150 at 5in for a cosy night.

Volume Volume is basically the thickness of the foam, with increased volume offering you more support. However, after a certain point volume is pointless, as a dense foam can have the same support at 3in thick as at 4in thick, depending on how you use it.

CHOOSING FOAM OR MATTRESSES FOR YOUR HOME CONVERSION

When the time comes to work out how big your bed is going to be in a home conversion, stick, if you can, to standard sizes, especially if you are looking at mattresses. While foam can be cut to size easily, it is extremely expensive to stray from standard bed sizes for some materials. So when planning your bed, stick to the following (in cm):

Sizing up your bed foam			
90 x 190	single bed	135 x 200/190	standard double
75 x 200	single bed	150 x 200	king size
122 x 200/190	small double	180 x 200	super king

MEMORY FOAM EXTRAS

Lots of campers like to top up their standard cushions with memory foam toppers, with the idea that a little extra comfort can make an uncomfortable bed more comfortable. And it can. However, in the camper van context, it does have limitations.

Memory foam has got a bit of a buzz about it. Everyone wants it because it moulds to your shape and cradles you in your sleep. It works very well in everyday life but its main property – that its hardness is determined by temperature – can work against it the moment you put it in your van.

Between room temperature and body temperature, memory foam will halve its hardness – it doesn't like the cold. So if you are creeping back from the pub to a cold van, it could well feel like sleeping on cardboard until your body temperature has warmed it up a bit. And if that memory foam is part of a multi-layered cushion (and therefore underneath a cushion cover as well as a sheet or sleeping bag),

Top tip for recovering rock and roll bed cushions

If you re-cover cushions for rock and roll beds, it is ABSOLUTELY VITAL to make sure that the cushions are fixed to the seat base if they are to be used with seat belts. Loose cushion covers can easily render seat belts useless as they can slide about in emergency stopping situations.

it'll take longer to heat up through your covers (if at all) and therefore longer to be effective (if at all).

Also, memory foam requires three-way fabric to be truly effective and mould to your body shape – this won't work through a vinyl covering. It's also bulky.

Tip:

Buy warmer than you think you'll need. You can make a hot sleeping bag cooler by opening the zip a bit but you can't make a cold sleeping bag any warmer on a cold night.

Sleeping bags, duvets, liners

Outdoor stores can be confusing places, right? Especially when it comes to sleeping bags and their ratings. What do they mean? And how can you measure? And, when it comes to duvets, what is a tog?

WHAT YOU NEED TO KNOW ABOUT SLEEPING BAGS

Sleeping bags are temperature rated. These are set by a European Standard (EN13537), which means that all sleeping bags must conform to the same standards and that the standards must be set in a predetermined laboratory standard test. The ratings are as follows, and they refer to someone with clothes on:

- **Upper limit/maximum rating.** This is the highest temperature at which you can sleep comfortably without sweating (based on a standard man, aged 25, with a height of 1.73m and a weight of 73kg).
- **The comfort rating.** This is the temperature at which a standard woman (25 years old, with a height of 1.60m and a weight of 60kg) can have a comfortable night's sleep.
- **Lower limit/minimum rating.** This is the lowest temperature at which a standard man can have a comfortable night's sleep.
- **Extreme rating.** This is the point at which the standard woman will be protected from hypothermia.

OK that's cool, or warm, or hot. But what about with jim-jams? Or what if you're not standard? Well, these ratings are given for the person with clothes on. They don't specify what kind of clothes, however, so your guess is as good as mine. I'll assume it's a pair of long johns and a T-shirt. How romantic. When it comes to standardness, it's also safe to assume that if you are skinnier than a standard man or woman, you'll feel cold more, while the reason they cite men and women is because of the fact that women and men react to temperature in different ways. Women generally (and this is not me that's saying it) feel the cold more.

WHAT BAG SHAPE TO GO FOR The shape and style of your sleeping bag will determine how warm it is. The rule is that the more air is inside the bag, the cooler it will be.

- **Standard/rectangular shapes** are standard in that they will fulfil your needs but may not be as warm as a mummy-shaped bag. BUT, on the plus side, you can zip two of them together to make a double bag. Handy, but not always.
- **Lozenge shapes** don't have the awkward corners of a standard bag shape so will still allow you to move about with a little extra warmth.
- **Mummy shapes** are the daddy, and will get warm quicker and stay warm longer. This is because there is less chance of colder air circulating, especially if you zip up tight and keep your head inside the hood. The shape can be restrictive for those who like to move about in the night.

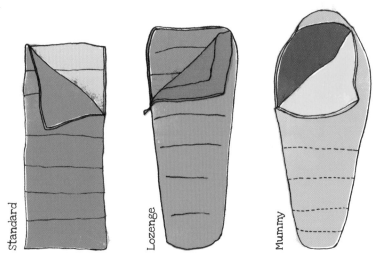

Standard

Lozenge

Mummy

For extra warmth and comfort, sleeping bag liners will add another layer and make it easier for you to keep the bag clean. You also get the added benefit of sleeping in a cotton sheet.

WHAT SEASON BAG TO GO FOR
To make it a little easier for the punters like us, camping stores divide their bags into seasons. These are as set out below and will allow you to make a choice. Remember, though, that the temperature ratings still apply here, so when choosing your bag you still need to think about when you'll be using it and what the limits you expect it to cope with are. Remember also that the extreme limit is less about comfort and more about survival.

- **One-season bags** are for use in a hot climate or indoor use.
- **Two-season bags** will see you through, as long as the temperature remains above 9°C. Basically, you're looking at a British summer.
- **Three-season bags** are for temperatures as low as 0°C and can be used from early spring to late autumn.
- **Four-season bags** are designed for winter backpacking or climbing. Useful for people who really feel the cold, but rarely useful in a well-insulated van.

DARN THE SAVING SPACE, GO FOR A DUVET
Very wise choice! A duvet is a far more civilised way of sleeping (especially with a friend), although you will need to carry a bottom sheet. The only downside is the bulk of them. Even so, you still need to be mindful of the tog rating. It's actually a lot less complicated than sleeping bags and it goes like this:

What's the tog rating? The tog is a measure of thermal resistance. That means that it's all about how a duvet will contain heat. So, for the layman: the thermal resistance in togs is equal to 10 times the temperature difference (in °C) between the two surfaces of a material, when the flow of heat is equal to 1 watt per square meter (eh?).

And that, in turn, translates as:

Summer duvet	4.5 tog
Spring or autumn	9–10.5 tog
Winter	12–13.5 tog

If you want my advice I'll say go for more togs than you think you'll need. You can always stick a leg out if you get too hot.

LOOKING AFTER YOUR SLEEPING BAG Stuff it in, that's it. No need to worry. You might think that stashing your bag away into its stuff sack is the best way to store it – but it isn't, apparently. The more compressed you make your bag, the more it's going to lose its insulating properties over time. So while it's OK to stuff it for short trips, store it in a larger bag between trips. If you fold and roll your bag the same way each time you'll stop the inner fabric becoming creased and working less efficiently.

Mosquito nets

On balmy nights it's a real pleasure to sleep with the tailgate open and allow a gentle breeze to cool you while you snooze away. It's almost a prerequisite of any camper van dream. It's hot. You can't sleep. You open the tailgate and listen to the sounds of the night. Everything is wonderful.

Until the insects find you.

The solution of course is to fit fly screens or mozzie nets to your van. They can almost always be retrofitted and are available for all types of modern campers. They can be extremely useful when travelling to areas where midges are prevalent.

Choose from full screens for sliding doors to tailgate screens. Or, if you don't want to go to that kind of expense, you can always use a standard mozzie net. They are generally cheap and will protect the bed only.

On-board heating

Whatever camper you own, there will come a time when your life would benefit from a little ambient warmth. It could be because you want to head north or just because you want to camp outside the summer season.

On-board heating, though costly, is one investment worth making. It extends the camping season – at the very least – and will make the whole thing a lot more civilised and fun.

If retrofitting a heater into an existing camper van, the most popular choice would be either an LPG Propex or petrol/diesel Webasto or Erberspächer unit. Petrol- or diesel-powered heaters draw fuel from the vehicle's fuel tank, so the heater's fuel supply is topped up with every visit to the filling station. Although more expensive, running costs are lower and fuel is more readily available. These heaters can also be thermostatically controlled and typically use around 0.1 litres of fuel per hour, making them suitable for all-night running.

DO NOT use the burners on a gas stove to keep warm. Prolonged use of a stove inside a closed camper van will gradually reduce the oxygen content of the air and then start to produce carbon monoxide, risking suffocation and carbon monoxide poisoning. Always carry a carbon monoxide alarm.

PROPEX HEATERS These are the easiest way to heat a camper and use a similar system to many other heaters. They are gas powered and create heat by combusting the gas in a closed combustion unit. Clean outside air is then heated via heat exchangers inside the unit before being blown into the cab of the van. Propex heaters can be controlled via a basic thermostat, which regulates the temperature and then cuts in when it drops. They are extremely effective when they work properly, but can be temperamental.

Propex heaters will run off both propane and butane but it's worth remembering the following:

- If you intend to camp in weather below around 5°C then you'll need propane.
- Butane, while burning more efficiently, will not convert to a gas below −1°C, so there will be no pressure in your gas bottle and therefore no heat, as there'll be nothing to combust.
- Butane generally comes in blue bottles and is characterised by Campingaz (it's actually a mixture of the two gases).
- Propane comes in red bottles and will work at temperatures as low as −45°C, which is why it's always been more popular for cooking and domestic heating.
- Most motorhomes will use propane, whereas the leisure camping market tends to rely on butane.

EBERSPÄCHER/WEBASTO This is another piece of kit that can be retrofitted to your camper van. They are popular in more modern vehicles and tend to cost more than the Propex heaters. They work in the same way as Propex heaters, with closed combustion and inlet and exhaust ports outside the van. The only difference is that they take fuel directly from the fuel tank (about 0.1 litres overnight) so you don't have to worry about extra gas bottles or the type of gas you use. The only thing to remember is to use it when you're not running on fumes, or you'll not go anywhere the next day.

BLOWN AIR Similar in how it works to Propex heaters, blown air heating systems are often the first choice of motorhome manufacturers. They have more features, such as hot water, hot water boost, a timer and the ability to communicate with your heating system via an app, so they are more expensive. The same principles apply here except they work off gas and electricity, so are useful on sites with hook-up. Gas, though, remains more efficient than electricity. So set the thermostat, get into your long johns and relax...

TRUMA CONVECTION These are gas-powered heaters and are similar to blow air heaters. They are popular with many caravanners and can even come with a gas fire effect. Get you, with your home comforts! These will require a flue to be operated safely.

WET HEATING SYSTEMS These are very similar to the heating system you might find in the home. The boiler (running off gas or electricity) heats up a liquid (water and glycol), which is then pumped around the vehicle through a series of radiators or in underfloor heating. It's very efficient and silent, which is why it's popular. Alde are the brand leaders.

WOOD BURNER For large home conversions, a wood burner can be a good alternative. It's also got a lot more personality! But it does come with problems, such as needing to make sure everything around it is heatproof, and that you have a decent fireproof hearth and a two-part flue to keep the heat away from the roof. You'll also need adequate ventilation and a carbon monoxide alarm. But oh those flames!!! Cosy

POWER

Camping electrics: leisure batteries

Most campers will have some kind of camping electrics, running off a separate leisure battery. They are 'deep cycle' batteries and are different from your average car battery because they're designed to be regularly deeply discharged, using most of its capacity. They have to cope with

a lifetime of being drained and then topped up instead of a burst (to start the engine) followed by constant topping up (from the alternator), as is the case for a car battery.

Leisure batteries are generally topped up via the split relay charger that delivers a topping-up current when the engine is running, and by mains charging when plugged into 240v hook-up, although not all campers have 240v chargers for their leisure electrics.

Different batteries have different ratings that are measured in amp hours (ah). This is the time the battery will run when drawing power measured in amps. If you have a 100ah battery and you run a lamp on it that draws 10 amps, the battery

will last for 10 hours before it is fully discharged. However, it is never recommended to discharge a leisure battery more than 50 per cent, as it may not recover fully. Therefore, it's important to get one that will be able to cope with the demands you place on it.

HOW TO WORK OUT HOW MUCH POWER YOUR CAMPER DEMANDS Every piece of electrical equipment in your camper will draw a certain amount of power, in amps. Multiply that by the number of hours you use it on average each day and add it all up together to get your power usage (so say a TV draws 2 amps and you use it for five hours a day, it will draw 10AH). Add up all the appliances and the time you use them for and you will get some idea of the size of battery you might need (leisure batteries start at around 75ah and go up to a whopping 170ah for more demanding motorhomes). However, since it is inadvisable to drain leisure batteries by more than 50 per cent, double your average usage to get an approximation of your power needs.

It's also important to choose a leisure battery that will fit your battery compartment. And bear in mind that all batteries must now be properly secured for your UK MOT.

Topping up with solar

Solar panels will enable you to keep your leisure battery topped up when camping away from a campsite or if you are parked up and not running the engine for a few days.

Which solar panel to go for is a bit of a minefield (as I found out when I started looking into it). However, there are companies out there who can help you make the right decisions about which set-up is right for you and your van. I sought the help of Colin from Select Solar, who very kindly gave me the benefit of his vast experience by passing on the following information.

In general, you'll need to choose a solar panel that will produce the same amount of power that you use each day on an average trip. That way, it will be powerful enough to top up your battery as you use up power the way you normally do. That depends on what kind of devices you have connected to your camping electrics. If you run an absorption fridge then it will require more power than a compressor fridge (for example), so you'll need more topping up power from your solar. Similarly, if all you ever do is charge your phone and use a few lights, something smaller – and much cheaper – will do.

TYPES OF PANEL There are two main types of solar panel: amorphous and crystalline. In general, amorphous perform better than crystalline under low light conditions and don't suffer as much power loss in hot temperatures. However, in good conditions, the efficiency of amorphous panels is lower, and they are physically larger than crystalline panels of the same wattage.

CALCULATE YOUR SOLAR POWER NEEDS You may already have worked out how much power you consume on a typical camping trip (*see* page 107), and therefore what size of battery you may need. So all you need to do next is to choose a solar panel that can produce as much energy as you use.

The power generation rating of a solar panel is given in watts. To calculate the energy it can supply to the battery, multiply the number of watts by the hours exposed to sunshine, then multiply the result by 0.85 (this factor allows for natural system losses). So, in four hours a 10w panel will produce = 34wh of energy to the battery.

Ready reckoner for solar panels

VEHICLE?	Camper van, caravan and small motorhome, 110ah battery	Camper van, caravan and small motorhome, 110ah battery	Large motorhome, 200ah battery	Large motorhome, 200ah battery
WHEN?	Spring–autumn	All year round	Spring–autumn	All year round
60w	Lights, water pump, radio and TV for 2hrs/day	Lights, water pump, radio and CD	Lights, water pump, radio and CD	Lights, water pump, radio and CD
85w	Lights, water pump, radio, TV for 3hrs/day and 240v appliances	Lights, water pump, radio and TV for 2hrs/day	Lights, water pump, radio and TV for 2hrs/day	Lights, water pump, radio and CD
130w	Lights, water pump, radio, TV for 5hrs/day and 240V appliances	Lights, water pump, radio, TV for 3hrs/day and 240v appliances	Lights, water pump, radio, TV for 3hrs/day and 240v appliances	Lights, water pump, radio and TV for 2hrs/day

SIZE YOUR SYSTEM The idea with a solar system is to balance the power going in with the power going out over a period of days or weeks. Here is a simple way to calculate the size of a system based on your power usage.

- **Find the wattage of your appliances:** If you can only find the figure in amps, multiply this by 12 to get the wattage.
- **Work out your daily watt-hour needs:** Work out how many hours you use an appliance per week, then divide it by seven. Multiply each appliance's wattage by the hours you'll use it in a day. Add the totals together for your daily watt-hour usage.
- **Work out your panel size:** Divide the daily total watt-hours by the hours of useable light in an average day. In the UK you can expect one hour in winter, rising to four hours in summer.
- **What do you need?** Most motorhomes have panels that are 80w and above because of the typical gadgets that get used (fridges, phone chargers, radio, lighting, etc.). Bear in mind that laptops require at least 25w for a useful trickle charge.
- **Work out what space you have:** Panels come in various sizes, shapes and ratings, so it may be possible to fit two instead of one if the size is right.

Lithium ion leisure batteries

This kind of battery can be useful if you want to remove gas from your van. They will allow you to run more powerful devices, such as microwaves and induction hobs. The benefit is that they deliver a consistent voltage all through their cycle, unlike standard leisure batteries, which means they will give you a better return over a longer period between charges. Depending on what kind of charger you install, they can also take a charge quickly. They can also be used with an inverter, so allowing you to charge laptops, e-bikes and camera batteries when off grid, or even when driving (if set up to do so). The downside is that induction hobs pull a lot of power so running a number of batteries can be a good idea. The downside is the cost as they are considerably more expensive than traditional batteries.

Cold weather battery performance

In cold weather the performance of a battery is reduced considerably (when you need it most), so it can help to have the leisure battery inside the van if you camp into winter. However, all lead acid and sealed-for-life gel batteries vent hydrogen as part of their normal working life so should always be in a separate compartment from the living space, and with a vent to allow hydrogen to escape.

Using a power inverter

Power inverters change direct current (DC) power from a battery into conventional mains alternating current (AC) power at 230v. This means that you can use one to operate all kinds of devices, such as your laptop, power tools or kitchen appliances.

The inverter draws its power from a 12v battery (preferably your deep-cycle camping battery). However, the battery will need to be recharged as the inverter draws out of it. You can do this by running the engine, with 10 minutes of running time per hour of inverter use being recommended. Most leisure batteries will provide an ample power supply for 30–60 minutes even when the engine is turned off, although actual time may vary depending on the age and condition of the battery, and the power demand being placed on it by the equipment the inverter is operating.

Again, see **www.selectsolar.co.uk** for more information.

Towing more kit

If you travel with a lot of kit, you might find it won't all fit in. Better get a trailer.

Trailers come in all shapes and sizes, weights and legal limits, so it's important to get it right. If you are a VW owner, your preferred trailer might well be a vintage Westfalia trailer or a cute teardrop trailer. Or even a Dub Box, a VW-inspired caravan trailer. For some, the look is all-important, but for others it's the space that matters. Either way, having more space separate from the van will give you much more flexibility and carrying capacity, and leave your mode of transport free for getting you around. Never mind reversing in the supermarket car park.

WHAT CAN YOU TOW? If you have a driving licence that was issued after 19 January 2013 and have passed a category B test (car and small vehicle), then you can tow a small trailer weighing no more than 750kg or a trailer over 750kg, as long as the combined weight of the trailer and vehicle is less than the MAM (*see* page 44). For towing heavier weights you need a further entitlement on your licence.

If you have a driving licence that was issued after 1 January 1997 and have passed a category B (car) licence, then you can drive a vehicle up to

3.5 tonnes towing a trailer up to 750kg MAM. You can also tow a trailer over 750kg as long as the combined weight of the trailer and vehicle is no more than 3,500kg. For towing heavier weights you need a further entitlement on your licence.

If you passed your test before 1 January 1997 you are entitled to drive a vehicle and trailer combination up to 8.25 tonnes MAM.

TOW BARS Tow bars must be type approved for your vehicle, must be designed for the vehicle and must meet EU regulations.

There is no need for type approval for cars first used before 1 August 1998. You must have an adequate view of the road behind you, therefore may require towing mirrors. If you tow without, you may be prosecuted.

TRAILER BRAKE SYSTEMS Any trailer weighing over 750kg, including its load, must have a working brake system.

NUMBER PLATES You must display the number plate of the towing vehicle on the trailer. This should also include lights and indicators.

TOWING CARS ON A FRAMES AND DOLLIES If you tow a car on an A frame (a rig that attaches to the car, keeping the four wheels on the ground) then it counts as a trailer, as does a dolly (a 'half trailer' that takes the front wheels of the tow car off the ground).

In the UK, the Department for Transport has strict rules about towing vehicles. They regard A frames and dollies as trailers, which means they have to comply with trailer rules as outlined opposite. These rules also state that if a trailer is fitted with a braking system, then the brake system must be operational. So your tow car's brakes must work in conjunction with your towing vehicles.

Dollies are mostly used for recovery but the law (in the UK) states that if a dolly is to be used for a functioning vehicle, then it must have a braking system working on the wheels that are on the ground. There are also other rules that state the upper limits for speed using a dolly are 40mph on a motorway and 20mph on other roads.

For more detailed information on towing in Europe, we recommend seeking further information from motoring organisations in the country in which you are travelling. However, please be aware that towing cars on A frames may be interpreted by some police as being against the law, for which you may be liable for a fine.

Condensation

Condensation is a common problem that affects all camper vans and motorhomes. Having condensation inside your van won't stop you from having a good night's sleep – unless it drips on you – because it is just a by-product of sleeping in a tin and glass box. But stopping it will make for a more pleasant experience all round and will mean you don't have to wipe the windows down each morning.

What's more, it can cause a real problem if the water hangs around for a while and begins to corrode the bodywork. If you allow it to happen a lot it could well kill your van.

WHY CONDENSATION OCCURS Whenever there are differences in temperature and moisture, condensation will occur. So, when you are cosy inside the van and breathing out hot, moist air, the likelihood is that you will create condensation if the outside temperature is different. You'll find it happens a lot more on cold nights.

Condensation can also be caused by high moisture content in the interior air of the van – from wet towels, using a shower, damp wetsuits, whatever. As long as there is a temperature difference it will happen.

STOPPING CONDENSATION Allowing air to circulate by opening a window or two will allow the moist air to escape and even up the temperature difference between outside and in. Insulating the van and windows will also help, as the insulation will provide a protective heatproof barrier between the two temperatures. Insulation will also help to keep the van warm and to stop warm air escaping through the thin metal sides of the van.

STOPPING WINDSCREEN CONDENSATION The windscreen is the place where you are most likely to get condensation. This is because it's a large area that isn't usually insulated. It's a pain in the backside to wake up every morning and have to wipe away gallons of condensation from a big windscreen, so anything you can do to alleviate the problem will be worthwhile.

Thermo screens that you can stick to the window interiors are a great idea that will stop a certain amount of condensation. Buy them or make them yourself with bubble wrap or foam insulation.

However, a more effective way to employ thermo screens is to use them on the outside of the van, so stopping the warmth of the van (and a nice warm windscreen) from having direct contact with cold air. These are available to buy, too.

Blocking out the daylight

Blocking out the light is kind of essential when it comes to getting a decent night's sleep. Or at least sleeping in once the sun has come up. So, getting the right curtains is important. It's also the first and most important soft furnishing you'll have to make decisions about.

Curtains can be about blackout or decoration or both. Most modern coach-built motorhomes will have some kind of blinds and fly screens so curtains are no more than a decoration to soften the edges a little. But for most campers, curtains are the way to go.

You can choose to match the interior and put up with whatever light-stopping properties they might have, line them and hope that helps, or go the full hog and make sure they are blackout lined. This will be more expensive, inevitably, but what price is a good night's sleep?

Curtain tips

- Magnets sewn into the linings can help to stop curtains from flapping about and letting in light.
- Velcro strips can be used to hold curtains together to stop light from coming in.
- Thermo mats can provide better light (and heat) insulation than curtains but have to be stowed away in the van somewhere. Curtains just tie back.
- Blinds are going to be more efficient than curtains at blocking out light, but are not as pretty.

LAST-MINUTE VAN MAINTENANCE

Before you set off on any trip it's smart to do a bit of essential maintenance in addition to the essential vehicle checks. Setting off fully confident that all is working and that you've done your best to avert disaster is not to be sniffed at. Happy holidays begin with a happy van.

Flush and fill fresh water

If it's been a while since you travelled then it's a good idea – actually it's vital – to freshen up the fresh tank before refilling. Even if you just carry a jerry can for fresh water, it's a good idea to sterilise it before using it again. If you have a water system in your camper or motorhome it is essential to flush it out and sterilise it before using it. This is because the build-up of bacteria in the tank and pipes over time can cause you to be ill, especially if your system has been left and it's been hot.

There are products on the market that can be used specifically to clean pipes, tanks and boilers.

Elsan Tank Clean or Puriclean are both used for flushing the freshwater tank.

Elsil is for keeping your freshwater tank fresh. It is recommended for keeping tank water safe to drink for more than 24 hours. If you worry about water quality and drinking from your tank, Elsil claims to make even the worst tank water drinkable.

Note: Do not use bleach or Milton Sterilising Fluid as it contains chlorine and that can damage stainless parts in Trauma boilers.

Some people use vinegar or citric acid as it will descale as well as sterilise and is not harmful to watercourses.

To clean and flush the freshwater tank:

- Empty the freshwater tank completely (open all the taps to avoid air pockets).
- Fill with cleaner using the proportions specified (or a cupful of vinegar/lemon juice per tank).
- Leave for the suggested length of time (run a little through all taps and shower first).
- Run the cleaner through the system by running all taps until the tank is empty.
- Fill the tank with clean water and flush through completely again.

Water tips

- Keep a large water container on standby for drinking water if you worry about drinking straight from the tank.
- Install a filter into your fresh system (if an option).
- If you are travelling a long way it makes sense to fill up with water when you get there or you'll just carry a heavy load of water for no reason.

Flush and freshen the waste tank

Waste tanks can stink, especially if it's hot. So if your van has been standing still for a while, flush it out. Using the same method above will flush it out before you go but do make sure that you empty it somewhere safe. To help keep it fresh put a recommended dose of Elsan's Grey Water Tank Fresh into the tank (pour it down the sink). Bicarb of soda will work too. Just put a little into the tank (via the sink) every time you empty.

Check the gas

Check your gas tanks are full or at least make sure that you know how much gas you have and where to get a refill or spare canister.

Test the cooker and heating to make sure that both fire up OK without issues.

Also check and test the carbon monoxide alarm and smoke alarm.

Check and charge your leisure battery

Leisure batteries can lose their charge over time, even if they are not being used. They also don't like being discharged and so need to be kept topped up. You can cause permanent damage to a leisure battery by letting it discharge too much before charging.

Use a voltmeter to check the charge on your leisure battery. Remember to disconnect it first. If it's below about 12V then it's considered flat.

If you have solar on your van, or use it as a daily driver, then you may assume that it's been topped up by use. Otherwise, it's a good idea to slow charge the leisure battery (with a smart charger) at least 24 hours before heading off. Some people keep their batteries on permanent charge by plugging into the mains when they are not using the van. This will stop the battery discharging naturally and dying on you.

Things that kill your leisure battery:

- Extreme cold.
- Leaving the lights on for long periods.
- Running a fridge off a leisure battery for long periods.
- Running in-tank water heaters for long periods without charging.

Check the fridge

Fridges, if left off for long periods, have a nasty habit of going bad. I am talking about mould and spores from old food. So don't leave it until you get there to check the fridge. Clean it out with your favourite washing-up liquid or kitchen cleaner and then run it for a bit while powered – by gas, mains or battery – to check it's getting cold and is good to go. In winter, use covers for the outside vents of the fridge (to ensure it works properly in low/ambient temperatures), and remove these in summer.

Charge the loo tank

Take a little peek into the loo – whether Porta Potti or cassette – and make sure it hasn't been left with anything nasty inside. If it has, or even if it hasn't, give it a good rinse out and charge up the flush tank with a little eco loo liquid. Check there's enough paper in the bathroom cabinet, too.

Final checks

Whenever you set off anywhere you might need to contain your giddy excitement just for a moment.

While you're probably excited to hit the road, whether it's setting off from home or setting off from an overnight, it's important to do a few last-minute checks. Think of them as the pre-flight checks. Always check the following:

- All cupboards are closed and locked.
- Drawers are closed and locked.
- Load is secure on roof rack.
- Step is retracted.
- Tickets, passport, money (have you left ID or a deposit with the campsite office?).
- Pop top is secure.
- Fridge, if 3-way, is set to battery and NOT running on gas.
- All skylights are closed.
- No items or rubbish left on the pitch.

Cabin doors to manual! Here we go.

Part Three

ON THE ROAD

Slide open the door and smell the warm air on the breeze. Feel the damp grass under your feet as you take your morning coffee, cupped in both hands, to a seat at the edge of the water. You can sit here and enjoy a few moments before the rest of your family wake up and demand breakfast, or your partner discovers you're missing or the rest of the campsite rises and yawns around you.

Savour it.

Why? Because it might not always be like this.

There will be days when the midges devour you, when you wake up at the side of a major road, when you can't find a decent pitch for love nor money or need to feel safe. It happens.

Life isn't one long Instagrammed #vanlife adventure with perfect people doing perfect things, looking out over mountains or making a fortune being an influential digital nomad. At least my life isn't. Often, it's about making decisions to stop or carry on, looking for somewhere to stay, going to the shops, having a day to do laundry or slopping out the Porta Potti. It all has to be done.

Hence this section. It's been written to be used on the road, to help you make good decisions. And, in doing so, to help make those dreams come true, with humour, grace and pragmatism.

They are out there. You just have to go and get them.

THE COST OF CAMPING

Once you've got the vehicle and the kit to go in it, the cost of camping isn't going to break the bank. In fact, it can be one of the cheapest ways to travel, if you choose. Some motorhomers pride themselves on how cheaply they can travel or how little they can spend when they are away. And it is surprising how little splashing of cash you can get away with, if that's what you want or need.

Variables

Depending on where you go, your cost of transport will vary. Staying local will make it cheaper. Finding free days out can help to cut the cost, as can mixing it up by staying on Britstops to save money on a few nights. Cooking at 'home' can also save a small fortune if you usually go for slap-up meals at the local restaurant.

CAMPING FEES Campsite fees vary from site to site. Extras also vary. Some sites grade their pitches into standard or serviced, or even super-serviced/deluxe pitches, which means they have electricity (and maybe a water tap) as part of the cost. I have stayed on sites on the Côte d'Azur that also have black (toilet) waste emptying on the pitch itself.

Some charge for the pitch and then add extras on top. Other just charge you for the night, irrespective of the number of people. Those are generally the smaller farm sites that might charge just £5 or £10 per night, for which you get a slice of field. Heavenly. The bigger, more organised sites may charge up to £50 (and beyond in some cases) just for the pitch in high season, with possible additions being the number of adults and children, whether or not you use electricity and if you have a dog or awning. Water and waste disposal should be free, but electricity may cost around £4 per night.

The other side of it, of course, is to wild camp where it is possible and legal, which means it's free!

WHAT ELSE WILL I HAVE TO PAY FOR? Apart from fuel, food or laundry, and perhaps days out, there's not really that much to it. Camping really can be a cheap way to take a holiday. But it doesn't mean you need to be stingy. Contributing to the local economy, even if it's just buying a drink, will make a difference. Buying your groceries in the supermarket before you leave and then spending nothing when you are there does nothing for the local economy and just helps to make a few shareholders in Surrey rich.

HOW TO SAVE £££ ON CAMPING Join a club, such as The Caravan and Motorhome Club (around £54 per year) to get access to Certified Locations, which are smaller sites with just five vans allowed on each site, at favourable prices. They cost around £15–£20 for a van plus two adults, a saving of £12 per night on non-member prices.

- Stay on a Britstop for free (*see* page 33).
- Travel out of season.
- Take bikes and save on off-site parking.
- Set a budget per day or night or week and stick to it. Staying on small sites could cost as little as £100 per week, whereas staying on big sites could cost as much as £500 (or more) in high season.

Budget for a week's touring holiday Mix it up a little and cook at home. Buy local and fresh. Stay on a mixture of cheap and expensive sites. Treat yourselves with a meal out! Add fuel.

Camping fees: one night on an expensive site	£70.00
Camping fees: four nights on a small site	£80.00
Wild camping/free aires/Britstops	Free
Food	£100.00
Eating out x 1	£100.00
Takeaway fish and chips x 1	£15.00
Days out/visits	£50.00
TOTAL COST	£415.00

HOW TO SAVE €€€ IN EUROPE

- Stay on aires. Some are free, others are no more than around €15 a night.
- Use a Camping Key Europe Card. It will give discounts on some sites at off-peak times and some discounts on peak season pitches too. These are available through camping clubs. **www.campingkeyeurope.com**
- Camp 'wild' where legal and possible.

TRAVEL SMART

Your smartphone is your lifeline when it comes to motorhoming today. With just the quick touch of a screen, it can instantly provide you with unlimited information. Aside from all the usual apps like Spotify, Twitter and on-demand TV, there are a bunch of specialist apps that will help you to navigate your way, save yourself and find a place to stay.

Useful apps

park4night is one of the most popular apps to use. It features more than 60,000 place all over Europe that are car parks, cafes, aires, campsites and wild spots.

searchforsites is similar to park4night and fast becoming the standard app. It is produced in association with Autotrail and, to its advantage, does have an online version for use when you are at home.

Facebook has just about every kind of group on it. There are a few that share overnights (whether legal or not). Campervan Overnight Parking has more than 110k members.

myLPG.eu is essential for finding LPG stations in the UK and Europe.

what3words could save your life. It divides the globe into segments, each with a unique set of three words. If you get into trouble then they will help the emergency services find you quickly and easily.

Caravan and Motorhome Club sites and Certificated Locations are marked on this easy-to-use app. UK only. Club membership required.

Motorhome Parking Ireland is useful for the Emerald Isle, pretty much useless everywhere else.

magicseaweed is a great app for surfers but also very useful when it comes to tide times and heights, daylight hours and weather.

PetrolPrices compares prices at thousands of petrol stations across the UK if you're looking for a cheaper fill-up.

ECO-CONSCIOUS CAMPING

If there is one message I'd like you to take from this book it is this: leave it better. What I mean is that we should leave anywhere we stay – a campsite, wild spot, wherever – nicer than it was when we arrived. You might also say that it should be a motto for the way we live in general.

One thing that sometimes gets forgotten – particularly by those who leave the remains of their picnics on beaches or who release their black waste into roadside gullies – is that the whole point of camping and motorhoming is to enjoy the natural world. So it makes sense to help preserve it, conserve it and even help to repair it so you may continue to enjoy it and other may too after you have gone.

I find it very distressing when we forget that we are part of the environment and depend on it for everything. It isn't there to be exploited, overcome, dominated or used up. It's there to support us, as if it were our own fluttering heart.

This section is about that. It's about trying to work out how to camp and live, in the way we love, without doing too much damage to the environment. In some cases, helping to repair it.

The greenest kind of holiday?

Motorhoming and caravanning and camping in general have long been recognised as a greener way to take a holiday. It might not be as green as cycling, walking or taking the train, but compared with flying it's looking very good indeed, especially if it's in a vehicle with a modern engine, driven carefully and parked up on site.

Pitch up carefully

This is the key. And it applies to all kinds of pitches. Whether you're pitching up on a beach in the Outer Hebrides or settling down for a night on a campsite in the south of France, the choices you make can have a lasting effect on the environment.

STAY ON SITES WITH GREEN CREDENTIALS If we are to take our leisure time seriously then we need to see it last. Supporting campsites that win awards, have incredible green policies, ban plastics or even use long drop or inventive toilet facilities should be supported. When they are successful, others will follow. Don't make the bad guys rich.

The David Bellamy Conservation Award is a badge that is given to the best sites and touring parks for outstanding work for the environment. To gain the accreditation, parks must manage their land as a haven for wildlife, reduce their use of energy, water and other resources, reduce, reuse and recycle the waste they produce and support their local communities

ENCOURAGE OTHERS TO DO BETTER If you stay on sites where bad practice is rife, talk to them about it. If they don't listen, don't go there again. You could even consider writing reviews asking them to make positive changes.

EDUCATE YOURSELF ABOUT THE PLACES YOU GO
I often use parking up on a beach in the Outer Hebrides as an example of why it's important to understand a little about where you are going, because parking up on a beach in the Outer Hebrides is an idea that many aspire to. I've done it myself. And yet the Outer Hebrides is home to one of the rarest habitats in the world – the machair – which is home to insectivorous plants, rare orchids and all kinds of fabulous blooms. And yet campers drive on it, eager to live the dream, not realising they are killing the dream at the same time.

So, if you can, find out about where you are going. Be careful where you stray from the path and do it in such a way that you won't damage anything there.

Be green yourself

The fastest way to reduce your impact is to be green yourself. I will talk about this later in more detail but it's about reducing your waste, being considerate, helping to repair nature and being unapologetic for it. And it starts with the basics:

- Drive considerately, keeping your mpg up.
- Reduce the waste you produce.
- Cycle or walk a bit more.
- Stay in one place longer than you might normally.

Stop blaming everyone else

A lot of people argue that there are too many people in the world, or that China's causing the air pollution, or that Indonesian rivers are responsible for the plastic in the ocean. It may be true (to some extent) but it's important to remember that we also pollute and that it doesn't mean you can do nothing. Everything we do matters, and the sooner we quit blaming everyone else for the mess and start dealing with our own, the quicker things will get done.

Leave it better: pick up litter

Picking up litter is an amazing thing. It can make you angry, sad and despairing but it can also make you feel very, very good. Picking up litter can be a catalyst for bigger changes and is a really good way of saying to those who might judge you that you care about the planet and are a responsible camper. Tidying somewhere up and seeing the result is instant and refreshing. I love it.

So, please, when you arrive and before you leave, do a sweep of your pitch (wherever it is) and tidy up. If you leave somewhere and there is a mess (even if it isn't yours) we will all get the blame for it. And the consequences of that are that there will be fewer and fewer places where we are welcome. Height barriers will go up, rocks will appear on lay-bys and the dreaded 'No camper vans' signs will breed like rabbits.

Forget single-use plastics

Everything comes in plastic these days. Salad, bananas, cucumbers, water, hummus, potato salad. It's frankly ridiculous the amount of packaging that our supermarkets and food stores force on us. Even when we don't need it. It's almost as if bananas, cucumbers and apples didn't have a natural protective outer casing on them.

So if you can, please stop using the single-use plastics. The problem with them is that they don't biodegrade, they turn toxic in water and break down into microplastics that will, in time, hurt us all. When you think about it, it doesn't make any sense to use a piece of plastic to carry your food home and then discard it. Unless, of course, you consider your personal convenience to be more important than the environment.

I realise that it's not easy being green sometimes, but there are choices we can make in the way we buy our food that can have a positive effect on the places we visit, so helping to make them better, too.

TAKING YOUR FIRST PLASTIC-FREE STEPS Buy loose fruit and veg where possible. Go to the deli counter with used and washed takeaway containers to buy ham, meat and fish.

- Cook from scratch when you can.
- Take your own mug or reusable cup for takeaway coffees and teas.
- Carry a water bottle and get a refill (bottled water is 500 times more expensive than tap and 95 per cent of it has plastic in it. Plus, Europe's tap water is the best in the world, though marketing tells you it's not.)
- Carry a reusable shopping bag whenever you visit a supermarket. Consider also using reusable vegetable bags for loose fruit and veg.
- Refuse plastic at takeaways and in restaurants (we're talking straws) and, if necessary, carry a spork or fork that you can wash and reuse.
- Try out a zero-waste shop for buying your staples, such as flour, pasta, cornflakes, nuts, rice and herbs.

Buy local when you can

Buying local food, from local producers, markets and shops makes so much sense. Why? Because if it's been grown locally by local producers

it's putting money straight into the local economy. You'll also get super-fresh produce that hasn't been halfway around the world or grown in countries where food and labour standards might be lower than ours.

Less waste: more recycling

Recycling isn't the answer to our packaging problems, but it's a start. So it's important to do it, if only to show others how it's done. Any campsite worth staying at will have recycling facilities. Please use them and get into the habit of separating your rubbish. Of course, it isn't always easy as recycling varies from one county and country to another but a little research will help.

Recycle as much as you can and if it can't be recycled, do without it.

Help your site - create less waste

Campsites have to pay for the waste that they (you) produce because they have to pay business rates. So the less waste you produce the less they pay and the less has to be collected and taken away. It's a very simple solution!

Help regenerate

Once we've cleared up the mess we've made, the next thing to do is to start regenerating what we've lost. When I travel in my van I 'offset' my travels by contributing to planting trees. I've done this while researching the last two books I have written and will do it for this book, too. It doesn't cost a huge amount (about £50 to plant trees to offset 10,000 miles of driving) but will help to compensate the planet for the emissions I create.

Can you go there?

Air pollution is a major problem in many cities across the UK and Europe. Tackling it, and making life easier for the residents, has been gathering pace across many European cities since the EU Air Quality Directive 2008/50/EU came into force.

The result is low emissions zones (LEZ), congestion zones, pedestrian areas and super blocks. It might not help us as drivers but it certainly helps those cities cope with overpopulation, pollution from vehicles and congestion, so I'm all for it.

But how do you know what's in place where? And what will happen if you fail to comply?

Some cities implement controls at certain times of the day, at weekends or for certain types of vehicle. Non-compliance can result in fines. And, thanks to the EU, these fines can now follow you home.

There are number of websites that list all low emissions zones and let you know what you need to do to comply.

www.urbanaccessregulations.eu is a site run by the EU and has links to the relevant cities and countries. Search by map, country or city.

www.green-zones.eu is a site that keeps up to date with current LEZ legislation. You can order stickers for your vehicle via the site.

STAY CONNECTED

I know you can't live without the internet, even though you try. I know your kids can't live without the internet. The great news is that you don't have to. And especially on the road.

Your phone, of course will give you access to the internet with 4G or 5G but there are ways you can set up your van as a mini-hotspot (without using your phone) or even like the international space station with more tech than Google.

Why internet is more than useful

I am sure I don't need to point it out but wi-fi is very useful in a van. When it comes to planning routes, paying for tolls or congestion charges (in Ireland for example, you can only pay the M50 charge online), searching for campsites, using apps and generally looking for information to improve your trip, it's really useful to be able to use a laptop or tablet rather than a phone.

WI-FI DONGLES The simplest way of getting internet in the van is to get yourself a wi-fi dongle and buy a SIM card with a data package. You can

simply walk into a phone shop and pick one up. They will allow you to connect a laptop or phone as easily as if it were your home wi-fi. Simple, and relatively cheap. The downside is that they are affected by the walls of the van so often work best when left on the dashboard or balanced precariously on a skylight.

ON-BOARD WI-FI Dongles have one disadvantage in that they rely on a good signal to get good speeds. Often, you may find that your phone may get a better signal. The way to get around this is to fit a wi-fi booster or antenna and router. A booster will improve a wi-fi signal in the motorhome, if there is one. So, it could be useful for staying on campsites, especially if the walls and roof of your van serve to block the signal. These can be deployed only when needed and removed when driving.

A 4G or 5G antenna and router will pick up and amplify any 4G or 5G signal and boost it (as well as wi-fi signal), which is very handy for off-grid camping, although a lot costlier than a dongle. Typical costs are around £300–£400. The aerial mounts on to the roof of the van and connects to a router inside. It is powered by your 12V battery or 240V when plugged into EHU. This will amplify the signal, creating a wi-fi hotspot inside the van. All you need to power it is a data-only SIM. Some makes will also boost a wi-fi signal on a campsite automatically.

Check out **www.motorhomewifi.com** for more information.

Smart vans - teching up your moho

On page 139 I talk about texting a smart heating system in the van to put the heating on. But you can go so much further than that if you want to. You can set up your wi-fi to work with a voice command system like Alexa, Siri or Google Voice to perform commands in the van, such as put security lights on, record CCTV, set the alarm, change the music or up the ante with a change of mood lighting.

In time, you may well be able to do all the same kinds of things that you can do with 'the internet of things' already in your home. Wouldn't it be great if your shopping, which your fridge ordered for you because you were getting a bit low on something, turned up on the campsite, all paid for and sorted? Or would it? ... (See my earlier comments about shopping locally!)

FINDING BETTER OVERNIGHTS

Once you've left home and hit the road you may not have the time to do as much poring over books, maps and websites that you can do before you leave. After all, there are chores to be done, such as driving, having fun and sourcing and cooking food. Now that you are wandering, these things are your job and finding a good place to stay is a part of it.

Unless you have booked every stopover in advance, the subject of 'where are we staying tonight?' will come up regularly. If this is the way you travel, then here are some tips. Options for overnights are on pages 136–137.

START EARLY Don't leave it too late to start thinking about somewhere to stay, unless you are prepared to drive into the night. In summer, around 4 p.m is a good time to begin considering it. It'll give you time to get there, chock up and settle before you start preparing food. In winter, think about it earlier or plan a day ahead.

DON'T BE FUSSY If you like to find the very best places to stay then make sure you've got a plan in place in advance as busking it often ends up with you having to accept second rate. Then again, last minute can also lead to fantastic night stops.

ASSESS WHAT YOU NEED Often, stops are dictated by what you need. Do you need food? Do you want to eat out? Do you need to service the van? Do you need to fill up? Do you need a shower or to do washing? What does tomorrow look like? All these are factors that will help you to make your decisions.

HAVE YOUR RESOURCES READY You may use an app like park4night or a favourite campsite directory/book. Keep these handy, in a glovebox or door pocket, so the co-pilot can access them while you drive. In time, you'll get to know what works and what doesn't and which to check first.

BE OPEN-MINDED If sites are full or aires and Britstops are not up to expectation, it's no biggie to pitch up, go to bed and then head off early the next day. Sometimes this can be a better option than driving on in the hope that the next place will be better. It may not. Stay cool and decide how tired/hungry/grumpy you are.

BE PREPARED TO STOP If you pass somewhere that looks amazing, be prepared to stop, even if it's too early. Well-located campsites or wild spots are hard to come by and one that looks incredible, with a pool, river or something special about it, is worth stopping for, even if it's before time.

Campsites Sites may close early or be full. So phone ahead if it's getting close to the shutters-down time. Check they have space. Some sites have late arrivals areas for when the barriers are down and reception is closed. The Caravan and Motorhome Club sites usually request that members arrive by 8 p.m, unless prearranged.

Service stations Staying overnight at motorway services can be a good option if you are really stuck and it's late. But bear in mind that you'll usually end up with a fine unless you pay a parking fee. Also, some service stations in Europe are not considered to be safe places to stop.

Wild camping Finding a good wild camping spot is not as easy as you'd think. Unless you are prepared to take risks and stay at the side of the road or in a lay-by then the chances of finding somewhere that's suitable are slim. However, there are always ways and means:

- Be prepared to be moved on.
- Look for somewhere you can tuck the van away.
- Avoid places with 'no camping' or 'no overnight parking' signs.
- Look for people to ask locally.
- Look at what other people are doing.
- Ask other motorhome drivers if it's OK.
- Don't share it with anyone else.

Pubs and Britstops Pubs stay open late so are less fussy about when you turn up. It may be wise to phone ahead rather than chance it. If you turn up and pay for a meal it may be worth asking if you can stay overnight.

CAMPING IN THE WINTER

Winter is the time when a good camper van or motorhome really comes into its own. You can stretch out the camping season and stay warm and dry when all around is chaos, snow, ice, wind and rain. Vans can make an adventure and a cheap skiing or snowboarding trip very possible. For kayakers, climbers, bikers, surfers, walkers and runners, the camper van becomes a cocoon in which to warm up, hang up the kit to dry and enjoy a few home-from-home comforts before the next day's adventure. Extra kit to carry:

- Anti-slip mats
- Snow chains and a mat to lie on
- Bucket for your grey waste
- Shovel or folding spade
- Soft broom

WINTERISING THE VAN Some vans and motorhomes come ready to roll in the winter when you buy them, but the chances are that, if you are buying new, you'll need a 'winter pack', which will cost extra. Winter packs include insulation for the fresh and waste tanks, wheel arches (on some models), blinds instead of curtains and tank heaters. All these things can be sourced separately if you are retrofitting.

WINTER TIPS

Plan your overnights ahead of time. In winter a lot of campsites are closed, with only a handful offering year-round pitches. Check in advance, even if you intend to wild camp (or use aires) as they are always useful for emptying tanks and filling up with water. A visit to a warm washroom and to service the van in winter at a good club site can be a godsend. Some sites even have boot and kit drying rooms for use in winter.

Use diesel additive. Diesel fuel can gel at low temperatures (around −12°C), forming a sort of wax in the fuel lines that, ultimately, can stop the engine from working. Some garages in cold countries use gel additive in their fuel in the winter, so filling up at altitude can help. Either that or use a fuel additive in the tank. Additive is cheap and easy to use: just put it in the tank.

Petrol is less of a problem at low temperatures, except when it comes to real extremes.

Fire up the heating. Truma's iNet heating system will allow you to text the van before you get back to it to fire up the heating. It's a real luxury but why not? Waiting for the van to heat up after a day on the slopes can be torture.

Cooking with gas. Propane does not vaporise (turn to gas) at −42°C (the boiling temperature), whereas butane will not vaporise at −2°C. Below this temperature, butane will be useless, which means that any cooking, refrigeration (keeping the beer cold) or heating will have to be done with propane.

Freshwater tanks that are inside the van will stand a much better chance of staying liquid than those that are underslung. Underslung tanks can be insulated and some have elements installed to prevent them from freezing. However, note that heating elements can drain a battery quickly.

Waste tanks can also freeze. A good way to avoid this (other than insulating the tank and heating it) is to open the drain and place a bucket beneath it. Any waste will freeze in the bucket and not in your tank or pipes.

Keeping the battery well topped up can be an issue in colder temperatures. If your leisure battery falls below a certain voltage (around 10V) then most types of heating won't work. Fridges can drain batteries, as can elements in waste tanks and leaving lights on. Additional temporary solar panels (they can be integrated into insulated window screens) can add extra top-up during the day. Keep an eye on the voltage and run the engine or go for a drive if it's starting to get low. Better still, plug into electric to charge up, if possible.

Condensation can be a problem. Making sure you have at least a little ventilation will help to stop it forming on the inside, even if it's freezing outside.

Take extra blankets as a precaution because, while heating is generally reliable, you may find it cuts out or you run out of gas unexpectedly, especially if your leisure battery dies.

Set up a drying room in the bathroom. In lots of vans the bathroom can become the warmest space (because it's enclosed) and therefore the best place to hang up wet kit. Also, it doesn't matter if it drips!

Retrofit heating. In smaller vans it is possible to retrofit heaters that run either off the petrol or diesel tank (Eberspächer heaters), or run off a gas bottle (Propex heatsource). They will need to be fitted by an expert as they have intake and outlet pipes, and can also be set up to work as you drive (if your van's heating is rubbish).

Exterior window covers can be useful when it's icy or snowing. They remove the need for scraping and can also provide extra insulation.

Pop tops are possible to insulate with custom-made wraps by the likes of Campervan Couture (**www.campervancouture.co.uk**), Rainbow Screens (**www.rainbowthermalscreens.com**) and others.

Carry a broom to sweep snow off the roof or windscreen after heavy dumps. Snow build-up can turn to ice on the roof, which can cause damage, will affect the efficacy of your solar panels and may cause a danger to other road users when you drive away. If your van is tall, take a telescopic ladder.

Take pegs. If you don't use an exterior screen, pop pegs under your wipers to stop them from freezing to the windscreen.

Snow chains are really fiddly to put on. Have a test run in good weather before you leave. In snowy conditions you'll get wet and cold lying on the ground to put them on: hence take a mat to use! Knee pads may also be useful. Don't drive too fast with chains on, 30mph max is usually recommended, and keep the driving style very relaxed with no fast slowing or speeding up.

KEEPING COMFY AND WARM

STAY WARM, STAY HAPPY

Anyone who has known bitter cold will understand the need to ensure you stay warm, dry and happy on any camping trip. And anyone who has woken to ice on the inside, a dripping nose and ice blocks for feet will appreciate the value of good socks, a good coat and, when necessary, a decent emergency blanket.

Apart from the fact that it can be dangerous to allow yourself to get cold, it's just not any fun to be cold on a camping trip. However, with the right gear, a cosy space to return to and the promise of a hot cuppa, it can be an awful lot of fun camping out in the cold.

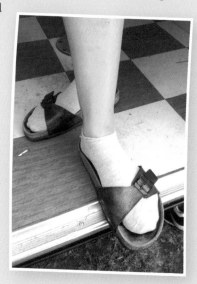

COLD WEATHER ANYTHING? BUY WELL
Buying once and buying well is the secret to a happy – and clutter-free – life. And all the more so when it comes to wet and cold weather gear. It's the same for sleeping bags. Spend a little more upfront and you'll invest in gear that will last.

BUY GOOD SOCKS Decent socks are hard to come by these days. But if you want to stay happy in the cold, your socks are the single most important piece of camping gear (almost, IMHO). Once cold hits your feet it's all over so don't scrimp on the socks. Keep fibres natural and consider the extra expense of merino, alpaca or good old-fashioned wool.

Merino is antibacterial (so you can wear it every day for a few days and not stink up the place), it actually heats up when wet (so even if your feet get wet they won't get cold) and it is soft. Merino also wicks water away from the body when you sweat, so won't stay wet. Likewise alpaca and wool.

Wool is also harder wearing so it will last longer than rubbish cheap socks – so enabling you to justify a higher initial price tag.

BUY DECENT BOOTS Again, don't scrimp on the footwear, for reasons outlined above. Decent boots will pay you back many times over when compared with cheap shoes, trainers or sneakers. Gore-Tex, like well-treated leather, will breathe and be waterproof for a long time.

GET A GOOD WATERPROOF COAT I like waterproofs but I don't like it when they sweat or weigh a ton. So, again the message is to invest in good waterproof rain gear that uses as few chemicals as possible.

INVEST IN LONG JOHNS Long johns will make a cool night warm. Surprisingly effective, a good pair (preferably Merino) can make a massive difference to any camping trip. They can even be worn under a pair of shorts if you get caught out being optimistic.

For cool nights, go for cotton. For cold nights, it has to be Merino or silk.

LAYER UP Layering enables you to regulate better as you can take layers off when you get too hot and put them on again as you cool off. There is a lot to be said for a super-warm Arran or Fairisle sweater, but it's either boiling hot on or freezing cold without. Layering gives you control. Natural fibres will breathe. Merino wool is great for technical gear and won't last forever when you cast it aside after long years of use.

GO LIGHTWEIGHT BUT WARM I have a jacket that weighs practically nothing but keeps me really warm in all but the coldest weather. It's not waterproof but I have an outer shell for that. This coat also packs down really small, is super light and makes a really cosy pillow. It's the ultimate two-in-one camping coat.

FINALLY, LOOK AFTER YOUR KIT... and it will look after you. Don't throw it away when it gets a rip. Mend it and love it for as long as you can. Some companies offer repairs of technical gear. Plus, visible mending is cool.

LPG and gas filling

Whatever fuel you are using to cook and keep warm, you'll need to refill at some point. Bottles are generally available all over Europe, but LPG can be an issue. Refilling LPG tanks is relatively straightforward, although the procedure can differ depending on where you are. You may have to pay in advance, ask the cashier to zero the counter or even ask the garage to do it for you.

Tip

When filling LPG in service stations, go and talk to the cashier first before attempting to fill up.

- Make sure you have the correct adaptor for the country you are travelling to. Find out what you need at **www.mylpg.eu/adapters**.
- Refillable bottles for LPG are available from Gaslow, GAS IT and Safefill, which replace the returnable bottles. There is even a handy Gaslow bottle for smaller vans.
- Beware that it is illegal to refill some types of gas canisters in France. Only cylinders that are EN1949 European Standard compliant may be refilled.
- Campingaz is widely available in Europe.

FINDING LPG STATIONS It's not always easy to find stations to fill up with LPG. I use **www.mylpg.eu/** as they have a map and an app, which will help you locate your nearest station. It's not a bad plan to keep an eye on your levels before you head off somewhere and make sure you can get gas if necessary. In some places you may have to drive a fair way to get to your nearest station. In winter, if you are running heating from your tank, it can get used up quickly.

DRIVING SAFETY

Only a fool forgets...

The two-second rule is a great one to teach the kids if you are one of those rear-enders and tailgaters who spends too much time too close to the car in front. It's pretty easy. All you have to do is find a mark at the side of the road and start counting as the car in front goes past it. Count in seconds – 'one-and-two-and' – the time it takes for you to reach the same mark. If you get there before the two seconds are up, you are too close to the car in front. If the weather or visibility is bad, double it for extra caution. Simple.

The two-second rule provides a distance of one car length per 5mph, no matter what speed you drive. The faster you go, the greater the distance, so allowing you enough time and space to be able to stop if something happens to the car in front.

Using the two-second rule can help to reduce accidents or damage if a collision happens. It can also help to save fuel and will reduce brake wear. The chevrons on the road work in much the same way when you see them on the motorway

Defensive driving

Following the two-second rule can also help to ease congestion in busy traffic, particularly those infuriating stop-start motorway journeys. By keeping a safe distance between you and the car in front you can have a significant knock-on effect on traffic and keep moving. How so?

When motorways are busy and slow, little things can bring traffic to a standstill: someone braking, someone changing lanes, a lorry going slowly. People react naturally to brake lights by braking themselves, so starting off a chain reaction behind them. In really slow traffic this will bring a line of cars to a standstill.

By keeping a safe distance between your van and the car in front you can slow down gradually and keep moving, albeit slowly. If you can crawl rather than braking and stopping then the traffic behind you should be able to keep moving too. If you time it right you will reach the queue after they have started up again so you can continue slowly without braking, and therefore without starting up that chain reaction of panic braking behind you.

Try it. You'll be surprised what kind of an effect your driving can have on the rest of the traffic behind you; even if it does nothing for the traffic itself it's better to keep moving than not move at all.

Driving safely tips

- Adjust your mirrors and seat before you set off.
- Keep hydrated and make sure you eat on long drives.
- Take regular breaks to get out and walk around.
- Stretch well during breaks.
- Break down your journey into segments.
- Stop as soon as you feel tired.
- Be extra aware at dusk or dawn.
- Wear the correct glasses.
- Keep your windscreen clear.
- Don't tailgate.
- Don't get distracted by your mobile phone.
- Don't drive on cruise control for long periods. Vary it a bit.

The obvious

From time to time I read things online that make me weep for humanity, especially when it's about motorhoming and campervanning. The most recent thing I read was a question from someone about baking potatoes in the motorhome oven while driving (so they are ready when you get there). Is it OK?

It's actually a perfectly reasonable question, if you don't know. But also one that had me shrieking at the screen. No!!!!! It is not OK. It's really dangerous to have the gas on when you are driving. There's risk of explosion, fire and personal accident.

On a positive note, the question actually inspired me to put the following list together. Just in case you have those kind of silly but maybe not-so-silly questions.

So peep out from between your fingers and read on.

I repeat: it's not OK to have dinner in the oven while you are driving. This is a huge fire risk. It is recommended that you turn off the gas supply completely while driving in case you have an accident and the gas escapes, risking an explosion.

It's not OK to put the kettle on while driving. Why? Fire and hot water spillage risk. Walking about in the back while not wearing a seat belt.

It's not OK to walk around in the back while driving (as a passenger). Why? It causes a risk to yourself and others if the van brakes or turns suddenly.

It's not OK to be in bed while someone is driving. As above.

It's not OK to use the loo or shower while driving. As above.

It's not OK for your passengers to eat at a table while you are driving. As above, plus the added hazard of flying food.

It's not OK to prepare food while you are driving. As above, plus the added hazard of knives.

It is not OK to do the washing up while driving. As above, plus the added hazard of water ingress into your units.

If you need to do any of these tasks, pull over and stop the vehicle.

Safety and seat belt law

The following information refers to UK law, with guidance from the Department of Transport. Seat belt law differs across the world so what applies in the UK may not apply where you are. However, the advice given in this book concerns the safety of you and your passengers. In that respect it can be followed wherever you may be. Just because there may be no law about seat belt safety in the country in which you travel, it doesn't mean you shouldn't heed safety advice. The consequences of ignoring advice are the same, whatever the law.

If you crash and you're not wearing seat belts then you are likely to suffer much more serious injuries than if you didn't. You may also injure others.

ADULTS When travelling in the front and rear, seat belts must be used if available. If they are not available, you are not obliged to used them. However, common sense says, don't travel if seat belts aren't available. It's not cool or clever to be dead.

CHILDREN In the front, all those up to 135cm in height (or 12 years or over, whichever comes first) must use the correct child seat/booster for their weight with no exceptions. If over 135cm or 12 years and above, they are treated as adults.

In the rear, where seat belts are fitted, then the same rules as for front seats apply but there are a few exceptions. If belts are not fitted in the rear, then those aged three years and above may travel unrestrained. Those under three must always use the correct baby/child seat.

SIDEWAYS FACING SEATS There is no legal requirement for seat belts to be fitted in sideways facing seats. However, in an impact those in such seats have an increased risk of serious injury. If seat belts are installed then they must be used by adults.

Children may not travel on booster seats or child seats facing sideways as their use prohibits it. Children may not use adult belts in sideways facing seats as they must be in the appropriate seats for their weight and age.

SEATS WITHOUT BELTS Adults may travel in seats without belts. However, my advice is don't. Besides, the police can take action against you if you carry passengers so that 'the manner in which they are carried is such that the use of the motor vehicle or trailer involves a danger of injury to any person' (UK Department of Transport).

INSURANCE AND NO BELTS What view does your insurance company have on passengers in your vehicle not using belts? If you have a crash and are sued for damages by a non-belt wearing passenger, will they support you? Think about it.

Likewise, if you are away from home and need medical treatment following a crash. Will your travel insurance pay your medical bills if they find out you were driving without a seat belt? It's important to read the small print.

REAR TRAVEL Although it is not specifically illegal to travel in the accommodation area of a camper van, you should bear in mind that this area would not have been specifically designed for use when travelling. You may be liable for prosecution (in the UK) if your manner of carrying passengers is deemed to be of risk to their safety or the safety of other road users. Basically, just belt up. That is all.

DRIVING IN EUROPE Under EU law, drivers and passengers must wear a seat belt in any seat fitted with one.

Children under 135cm tall, or travelling in cars/lorries fitted with safety devices, must use an approved device for their size. Taller children may use an adult seat belt. Rear-facing child restraints are no longer allowed on front passenger seats unless the airbag has been deactivated.

SEAT BELT LAW IN THE USA The laws in the USA differ from state to state, with some states only demanding that those in the front buckle up. In one, New Hampshire, there are no rules at all. If in doubt, buckle up.

SECURITY

Daytime security

Leaving your van at the side of the road, in a car park or at a beauty spot while you go off on your bike or to do your favourite sport is a risk. I've had my clothes stolen from a vehicle while surfing, for example. I also hear of others' vans being broken into and robbed while out. Not nice. So how can you avoid it?

- Don't leave anything visible and tempting for thieves. Keep all valuables out of sight.
- Don't park in isolated spots.
- Have a secret (lockable) cubby hole for all your valuables, such as passports, documents and cash and cards.
- Get an approved alarm and, steering lock and lock any bikes to the bike rack. Make it really difficult to steal them.
- Lock surfboards, kayaks and roof-based toys, if you can.
- Don't leave windows open. Open roof vents if it's hot.
- Don't allow access to ladders.

Overnight security

I occasionally hear horror stories of people being robbed while they sleep in motorhomes, particularly in Europe. It's horrible to think that someone might have the audacity to do this, but it does happen.

- Leave roof vents open, with fly screen across.
- Don't open cab windows, unless safe. Secure all other windows.
- Use the cab alarm.
- If you need to leave the tailgate open for ventilation, get a tailgate vent lock.
- Consider motion-sensitive security lights.

On-site safety

MIND YOUR HEAD!
If there was an injury typical of the camper van or motorhome owner it is banging the head on the door frame (getting into the van), and on a cupboard (when standing up too quickly or bending down to pick something up). Also at risk are those who forget where they are in the morning and get out of bed too quickly.

Top tip
In some vans and motorhomes it is possible to loop seat belts through door handles and then click them into place. This will make it impossible to open the doors from the outside, even if they are unlocked and the windows are partly open. Alternatively, you can buy a device that does similar from Fiamma if your seat belts won't go that far.

Head injuries can be serious. So, if you have hit your head hard and are knocked unconscious at all, seek medical help.

Concussion can occur if the head is shaken at any point. After a period of unconsciousness (usually less than three minutes), perhaps with vomiting after, signs of response improve and you should recover.

Compression is very dangerous and occurs when the brain is placed under extreme pressure caused by bleeding or swelling. Response worsens over time, even though recovery, at first, may seem to be normal. Seek help.

TRIPS, SLIPS AND FALLS

- When putting up an awning or a pup tent, be mindful of the way you peg out any guy ropes. Put them in places where they are obvious and use hi-viz ropes, if possible.
- Use a torch when walking around the campsite at night.
- Always carry a first aid kit in your van or motorhome.

CARBON MONOXIDE Carbon monoxide is the silent killer. And it is a killer that visits some campsite or other every year. There are rules about this: DO NOT EVER, UNDER ANY CIRCUMSTANCES, light a BBQ in a tent. This includes awnings or tent porches. It also includes BBQs that have been used and are still smouldering. They still give off carbon monoxide. No excuses.

- If you cook in your van, make sure there is always plenty of ventilation.
- Install a carbon monoxide alarm in your van TODAY.
- Service all your equipment (fridge, cooker) regularly.

FIRE WHILE COOKING Fire is a genuine risk in camp as we tend to be a little freer about it than at other times. So here are a few pointers for fire safety:

- Have you got a fire extinguisher in your camper? Get one.
- Also consider a fire blanket, which can be very useful for smothering cooking fires.
- If cooking over open fires or BBQs, do it where there is no risk of grass or scrub catching light. Only light a fire or BBQ with permission from the campsite owner.
- Cook well away from any awnings or tents.
- If you want to use candles, consider tea lights inside jam jars. If they fall over there is much less risk of fire spreading. Don't light candles inside tents or vans. Better still, use fairy lights.
- Avoid cooking with lots of hot fats.
- Extinguish any fire fully before you go to sleep. Never leave a fire smouldering.
- If you must have a fire, do it where it can be contained, for example, in a fire pit surrounded by stones, or in a man-made fire pit such as an old wheel or washing machine drum that is off the ground or on sand.
- Have a fire bucket full of water handy whenever you light a fire or BBQ.
- Don't use disposable BBQs as they are both wasteful and encourage littering.
- Don't leave your fire unattended at any time.
- All campsites should have fire points. Find out where they are.
- Don't pitch your tent or awning closer than 6m to the nearest neighbour. This helps prevent fires spreading.

BITES AND STINGS

- Carry insect repellent, antihistamine cream and allergy tablets in your first aid kit.
- Avoid mozzie bites by covering up.
- Treat weever fish stings with hot water.
- Use mosquito screens on windows and vents if you sleep with doors open.

CAMPING ON OR NEAR WATER Water of all types – pools, lakes, rivers and the sea – are potentially lethal to all of us. But they are more dangerous to small children than anyone, so it's vital to watch them at all times if you are near water. Get them swimming lessons at the very least.

On the river or lake

- Only swim if you know it is safe.
- Don't swim near fast-flowing water or near overhanging trees or branches.
- Don't jump into water unless you know how deep it is.

At the beach

- Only swim on lifeguarded beaches.
- Only swim between the red and yellow flags where the lifeguards can see you.
- Don't swim when the beach is red flagged as it means it's unsafe.
- If you get caught in a current, swim at 90 degrees to it, then swim in. Don't try to swim against it.

WARNING! If you, or anyone, has a near-drowning incident and has taken in water or been resuscitated, seek medical attention, even though they may seem OK. Secondary drowning (when a person has water on the lungs) can occur hours later.

KEEPING YOUR SPOT

What happens if you're on a campsite (or on an aire) and you decide to go out for the day? On sites where you have an allocated pitch it's obviously no problem as that pitch is yours for the duration. On other sites, where you can choose your own pitch, this can be an issue.

This is where awnings and pup tents come in useful. They can provide a secondary purpose of enabling you to mark territory and hang on to it.

Some campers also use windbreaks or a table and chairs, while others carry signs that politely point out that the pitch is taken, and may also include the number plate of the vehicle.

Of course, on aires you have absolutely no right to a pitch unless you are on it and it is unreasonable to expect anyone to leave it clear for you, even if you leave a sign or polite note.

REMEMBER: It is perfectly reasonable to expect others to pitch 6m away from you and you should also do the same.

Tip

Get a duplicate of your number plate, affix it to a metal spike or tent peg and bash it into the ground where you park. Then, when you go out for the day, other motorhomers and campers will know it's your spot.

LEVELLING WEDGES AND CHOCKS

Levelling wedges

Levelling wedges are wedges that you drive on to in order to level up the van. Chocks are blocks that keep you from rolling away.

Wedges are small but vital. This is because not all ground is level – especially campsite pitches. If you've ever tried to sleep on an incline, even a mild one, then you'll know that it's not the best way to get a good night's sleep. At best you'll spend all night tossing and turning. At worst you'll end up in a heap on one side of the van. If you have nylon sleeping bags, leather seats or even satin sheets (God forbid) this will be even worse and you may slide off the bed altogether. Levelling also affects cooking, eating and everything else in the van, too, so it's important to get it right.

The size of the wedges you need will normally be determined by the size of the van. Longer wheelbase vehicles generally need taller wedges as the height difference between back and front wheels is greater than on those with short wheelbases.

Levelling can be done by eye, with the aid of a spirit level or with a glass of water on a flat surface. How thoroughly you do this depends on how you sleep, whether or not you can be bothered or if you have a pernickety assistant.

Hand brakes, swivel seats and wedges

If you have a swivelling driver's seat and a handbrake that needs to be depressed to operate the swivel you might need a little help getting on wedges, staying there and swivelling the seats. Vans with floppy handbrakes won't have this trouble.

How to operate a swivel seat on wedges:

1 Drive up on to the wedges and set your heights.
2 Pull on the handbrake.
3 Keep your foot firmly on the footbrake and stop the engine.
4 Get off the seat, keeping your foot firmly on the brake and hanging on to the steering wheel. DO NOT let your foot off the brake.
5 Get an assistant to release the handbrake and swivel the seat then pull on the handbrake again.
6 Release the footbrake and step down.
7 Sleep like a baby.

AWNINGS AND SUNSHADES

Awnings come in three types:

1 Drive-away tent awnings that add another room to your van.
2 Fixed awnings that are permanently fixed to the van and that provide shelter.
3 A tarpaulin or sunshade that's not fixed to the van but fixes to the guttering or awning rail.

Awnings and pup tents

DRIVE-AWAY AWNINGS These are the type of awning that add an extra room and attach on to your van so that you walk out of the sliding door (or door) and into them. You can drive away from them, leaving them up like a tent, or they can be fixed to the van (more about that in a moment). Drive-away awnings are useful for the family that doesn't have enough beds or sitting space in the van itself as they can effectively double the living space of your van. As such they are used mostly by people driving smaller vans and are great for setting up beds or tables and chairs.

Drive-away awnings come in various guises, with the most recent innovation being the SheltaPod, an easy-to-assemble awning that actually looks very cool and was started thanks to a Kickstarter campaign! See more about this below.

AirBeam awnings are popular too, but tend to be heavy and take up a lot of space, even though they are a doddle to put up. Some, like Vango's AirBeam Rhone, are huge and can cost upwards of £1,200.

Standard awnings with poles can attach to the side door or, in some cases, the rear doors. They attach either with a pole that sits in the gutter (and get clamped into place) or with some kind of permanently fixed rail that the awning slides into (but can be a bit fiddly). Others rely on straps that go over the van (but aren't great for pop-tops). They are generally cheaper than AirBeams and don't get punctures. Expect to pay from about £250 to £800.

- In windy weather, make sure you peg out your guy ropes properly. Allowing an awning to blow away may cause damage to the van.
- Erect the awning with the van in place and level first, but make sure you leave space for the van to drive away.
- Don't put out guy ropes in the way of the wheels if you intend to drive it away.
- An awning skirt, which attaches to the side of the van between the wheels, can help stop draughts coming under the van and into the awning.
- Be careful when you open the sliding door as it can foul an awning and rip it.
- Accurate re-coupling is required to avoid slack joins and pools of water gathering!

Pup tents and event shelters Pup tents are little tents that people take with them to stash gear, teenagers and snoring partners. They can be useful if you have kids who want privacy or if you have brought so much gear that you want to leave some of it behind when you go out for the day. An event shelter is similar but with the added advantage that you can hang out underneath it too, when it rains. If you have space in your van then it can be a useful addition if you regularly suffer from overpacking syndrome.

The SheltaPod This is an extra room-cum-event shelter type of tent that can be used both as an event shelter and as an extra bedroom. Unlike most event shelters it can also be fitted with an inner tent to make a double-skinned bedroom. Handy! **www.sheltapod.com**

FIXED AWNINGS These kinds of awnings are the roll-out type and are attached to the van permanently. As such they need a little extra care during use. They can include a combination of sides and extra sections to make an extra room for the van but that does mean you won't be able to go anywhere in a hurry. It may be interesting to note that the DVLA now require the presence of an awning bar for a home conversion to be considered a motor caravan.

Also, it is really important to make sure that your awning is pegged out properly. When fully unfurled they have a huge surface area. Most awnings will come with some kind of strapping to use as an extra insurance policy. Allowing an awning to flap in the wind will cause damage to it and the van, which could ruin your trip.

- If you are using your awning to shelter from rain, make sure one leg is lower than the other. That way, rain will run off to the lower end rather than pooling.
- If possible, put your back to the wind.
- If it is windy, use straps to peg out the awning in addition to pegging the legs.
- Even if it's not very windy, peg out the legs to stop them from lifting.
- If it gets really windy, wind it in!

• If you cannot put pegs into the ground (because it's hardstanding), strap the awning to the wheels of the van using ratchet straps.
• If you are using the awning as a sunshade, make sure your van is facing the right way to benefit from it. Putting your sliding door (and sunshade, if on that side) to the north will get you the most shade. Likewise facing east will get the most shade in the evening, and west the most in the morning. Facing south will give you the least shade.

Awning skirts There is one annoying thing about awnings and that is the fact that wind blows under the van and into the awning, making everyone cold and making it billow. The way to avoid this is to use an awning skirt that connects between the two wheels of the van and blocks out any moving air, although a surfboard will work just as well!

Toilet and shower tents

Aka the latrine. These are pretty useful if you have a Porta Potti and don't want it in the van while you sleep. Handily small and packawayable for midnight visits when the loo block is just a stroll too far away or for when you're out in the wilds. They even come in pop-up form so you can wrestle them away when you've done your business. Now that's glamping.

Sunshades and tarps

These are a super-cheap option and can be very versatile, allowing, in some cases, any configuration of shade or shelter. Sunshades attach to the van either using a fixed awning rail or with a rail that goes in the gutter and clamps to it. It's possible to make your own or use something like Olpro's retro sunshade: **www.olproshop.com/products/shade-camper-van-canopy**

Batwing tarps can also be used to provide some kind of shelter, provided you have a way of connecting them to the van.

• Sunshades generally have to be put away when you drive away – they cannot be left up.
• Super-cheap option.
• Pack down small and neat so easy to carry.
• Useful for hot days or showers.

FIND YOUR ROUTINE – FEEL AMAZING

On your trips

Driving can take its toll on your back, especially if you're hunched over the wheel for hours on end, tackling stressful roads or sitting in traffic. Equally, sleeping in an unfamiliar bed in the van can upset your routine and leave you feeling stiff and uncomfortable.

I've had my fair share of bad back days, partly due to an injury to my back from years ago. It's taken me a long time to get to the bottom of it – osteoarthritis in my spine – and to manage it. But, I am happy to say, I can. Here are my tips for keeping yourself feeling good.

- Drink lots of water.
- Stop regularly and move about when you do.
- Keep a stash of something to nibble on nearby if you skip lunch or meals because you're driving. I always travel with a bunch of emergency bananas.
- Breathe deeply if you feel stressed.
- Remember that it is you who is responsible for your own health.

In the mornings

I do stretches every day to help combat the tightness and pain after a long drive or a difficult night's sleep. From feeling as if I was having a heart attack every day (caused by costochondritis) I now have chest pains and a bad back very infrequently. This is what works for me. You might have to find your own version, but start with this and start gently. See what a difference it makes. If necessary, go to a physio and tell them you want help so you don't have to come back. It's music to their ears. My physio set me up with the following, plus some I picked up along the way.

- **5 x Cat-Cow Pose:** On your hands and knees, bend your spine upwards as if you are a scared cat, with your head down. Then drop your spine and raise your head, as if you are a cow! Simple. Repeat 5 times and hold for 5 seconds each time.
- **5 x Thread-the-Needle Pose:** Stay on your hands and knees. Pass your right arm under your left armpit and reach, getting your right shoulder as near to the floor as possible. Repeat on the other side. Hold for 5 seconds each side.
- **5 x Child's Pose:** From a hands and knees position drop your bum onto your calves and allow your arms to spread straight out in front of you. Keep your head down. From this position, walk your hands in an arc 90 degrees to your right, keeping your arms straight, and hold, then back to the centre and then to the left and hold.
- **5 x Reach Stretch:** From a hands and knees position stretch out your right hand behind you as far and as high as you can reach. Turn your head to look at your outstretched hand. Hold for 10 seconds. Change arms and repeat.

KEEPING CLEAN

Personal hygiene

Sometimes keeping clean can present a challenge when you are out and about in a camper van or motorhome. If you have on-board facilities it's easier, obviously, but if you haven't it doesn't need to be a real issue.

For those who dare, washing in rivers and lakes is OK as long as you don't use detergents that will kill fish and damage the natural environment you have worked so hard to get to and enjoy. And that, perhaps surprisingly, means not using any at all. Or at least using, and disposing of it, well away from the river or lake. Why? Because soaps, even biodegradable soaps, break water tension and can cause algal blooms.

HANDWASHING This is important these days for all the usual reasons and more. Before preparing food, after going to the loo, after being out in shops or where there are other people, it's wise to use soap and water.

If you can't use soap, use an alcohol liquid. Don't use hand sanitiser gel – it's made with plastic.

Lake or river washing

- Fill a washing-up bowl with water.
- Dip yourself off in the lake or river.
- Use soap and detergent away from the watercourse (at least 200m).
- Wash with a flannel. Rinse off using the water from the bowl.
- Dispose of the water where it won't enter the watercourse directly.

Personally I am in favour of this 'leave it nicer' idea whereby our camping and campervanning has a positive impact on the environment.

So that means being as considerate with waste and detergents as you would with all your other waste, such as bottles, cans and plastics.

FOR CAMPERS AND MOTORHOMES WITH ON-BOARD FACILITIES

Washing in on-board bathrooms can present challenges, mainly due to space, but also water usage. Some are bona fide wet rooms and can handle a shower, while others are not so much.

Showering in wet rooms

- Be organised and quick.
- Expect everything to get wet.
- Make sure you have enough space in your waste tank.
- Use eco-friendly soaps.
- Soap on a rope keeps the soap in place!

Conserving water

- Use flannels to wash in a basin. Wash them regularly with laundry (or hand wash).
- Use different flannels for face, bums and pits.
- Hang flannels from pegs on a coat hanger to keep them separate and dry.
- Do not use wet wipes. They do not break down and often contain plastic.

Emptying grey water tanks

● **Grey water tanks** contain food particles and the residue of your washing up and washing and showering. Unless you use 100 per cent environmentally friendly detergents, soaps and toothpastes (normal toothpastes are particularly bad), your grey water can be harmful to the environment, water courses and wildlife.

● **Food particles in grey water** can help to attract rodents and scavengers if it is dumped at the side of the road, on a pitch or over someone's hedge.

● **Dumping your grey water tank** on your pitch, everyone agrees, is unsociable and leads to bad smells and unhealthy patches. So, don't do it.

● **Dumping grey water while driving** along is considered bad practice and unsociable. It may also lead you to a prosecution for polluting. It also gives us all a bad name.

● **Dumping grey water down a drain** at the side of the road isn't good practice. Unless you can guarantee that a roadside drain flows into the mains sewerage plant or into the mains drainage, it could pollute and cause harm to wildlife. Therefore, it's not good practice.

Dealing with grey water, best practice:

● Use a motorhome service point if there is one available.
● If there isn't one available, consider emptying your grey water into a container and disposing of it in approved drains or sinks.

FOR CAMPERS AND MOTORHOMES WITHOUT ON-BOARD FACILITIES Keeping clean in a van without a shower can be a challenge sometimes. But it is possible. Using a bowl and a flannel works well anywhere and ensures, at least, that you keep the vital bits sweet.

Baby wipes Tempting though it might be, don't freshen up with baby wipes. Unless they are made from biodegradable materials (not plastics) they contain plastics that will not disintegrate like toilet paper. If you flush them they cause blockages in the sewer system. And when you leave them in a hedge they will not rot down. Be suspicious of 'flushable' wipes, too. Some campsite waste systems cannot cope with them.

Solar showers Showering in the wild using a solar shower – great in Europe or on hot days – can be a bit of a laugh (I would recommend taking a bit of rope to hang it from an appropriate branch or tree). But avoid using soaps or shampoos, even if they are 100 per cent biodegradable. When you consider what some of the chemicals we put on our bodies can do to watercourses or plants, it's a wonder we use them in the first place.

Take a dip in the pool If you want to avoid campsites, then showers at a swimming pool, gym or leisure centre can be very useful to wash off the muck and grime. Some leisure centres will even allow you to pay for just a shower, which is perfect. It's the same with hot springs, spas and beach showers.

Service stations Those in the UK that are signposted from the motorway are required to provide showering and washing facilities for HGV drivers. You may have to ask for the key. I have used those at Tebay and Gloucester services and they are clean and well looked after.

Going to the loo

There are lots of good reasons for travelling with your own on-board toilet. For one thing it's very useful to be able to go whenever you need it. It's not always possible to find a public loo when you are out and about and it's a pain to have to trudge across a campsite in the middle of the night. In addition, if you are wild camping or aire camping in Europe then you will need to have one, as most places don't have facilities.

Porta Pottis and chemiloos Porta Pottis are self-contained camping toilets that have their own mini water reservoir for flushing and a container for the waste. They come apart and can be separated for ease of handling and cleaning. Chemicals are added to the flushing reservoir (often known as pink chemicals) as well as the waste container (blue or green chemicals) to aid cleaning and waste breakdown.

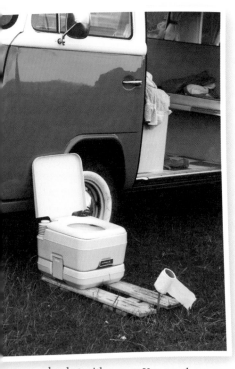

When buying chemicals for your Porta Potti you can choose eco-friendly products or non-eco-friendly, which are products that may be more effective but that can be harmful outside the contained usage of the loo. Some campsites will specify the use of eco-friendly chemicals only.

The advantage of a Porta Potti is that it can travel, even when used, so you don't have to worry about emptying it immediately after use. But don't leave it any longer than a day or two.

TIP: Make sure you have soap and water handy to wash hands after using or handling them.

Bucket and chuck it toilets Really? Yes. There are very simple products available that are nothing more than a bucket with a seat. You go, then you pour it away, but you wouldn't really want to be too far from an emptying point as it's not going to travel well. And you really can't just empty it anywhere (see the section opposite).

Toilet powders There are some products available that use powders to gelify waste in a biodegradable plastic bag. These are then put into a standard bin or compost. The advantage of such a system is that all the components pack neatly down and contain no water. It's all dry.

Spade and straddle If you must dig a hole (and you must dig a hole rather than not dig a hole), do it at least 200m from any watercourses, rivers, streams, paths or the sea, cover it up properly and restore the ground to how it was before you got there.

Cassette toilets These are the type of toilets you find in motorhomes. Some may have electric flushes and all kinds of luxury. These combine with an integral loo inside the vehicle. The cassette will usually be removed from the vehicle for emptying from a hatch outside the motorhome. The flush tank and waste tank will take chemicals like the Porta Potti.

TIP: Use green liquid for your loo as traditional blue chemical toilet liquids should not be disposed of in a lot of places, especially places with septic tanks and public toilets.

EMPTYING YOUR TANKS This is where it gets fun. On campsites all over Europe, at around 8 a.m. you'll find a steady stream of grim-faced men between the ages of 35 and 85 (it's always the men) strolling over to the 'slophopper'. Once there, they will make weak jokes about the day only getting better from here while they slop out the tanks with a stoical smile. There's a knack to it to avoiding unpleasant splashback, with some tanks having an air release valve to make for a better flow.

Anyway, the rules are that you do not empty your tanks into anywhere there is fresh water because it is a toxic mélange that must go into the

Drain for fresh water   Drain for grey water   Filler for fresh tanks

sewage system and be treated properly. It must not be emptied into drains, overflows or rivers. Some campsites will have special areas for swilling them out. Use them.

Loo paper It is recommended that you use special 'quick dissolve' toilet paper in chemical loos. This is because it will break down quicker and lead to less clogging. It's not the cheapest option but it does work. Alternatively, use thin, cheap paper as this will break down easily too. DO NOT use wet wipes in chemical toilets as they will not dissolve and will cause blockages that YOU will have to sort out.

Tip

Carrying a short length of hose, kept separate from your freshwater filling hose, will let you give your empty cassette a quick swill out before you put it back in the van.

Wash and brush-up stops

Part of the romance of travelling by camper van is that you have everything – water, cooker, fridge, food, heating and a loo – on board so you can live 'off-grid'. Lots of vans are capable of doing this for protracted periods, especially the larger motorhomes that have 150- or 200-litre freshwater tanks and huge fridges!

Aside from the issues of camping wild – the legality and practicality of finding places where you can stay – there are times when you need to wash properly, in a proper shower with space, hot water and all the regular comforts.

Even in Europe, where you can refill water and remove waste, you might struggle to wash clothes or get a proper shower. This is where campsites are worth their weight. Checking in to a campsite every few days – or even once a week – will allow you to spend a day servicing yourselves and the van:

- Empty and fill waste tanks.
- Wash and dry clothes.
- Shower and wash hair.
- Charge up the batteries ready for the next adventure.

Some people think it's cheating, but really, it isn't. It's being practical! And it's likely to cost anything between £20 and £40 per 24 hours, which, in the grand scheme of things, isn't much.

Getting your smalls done

If you intend to stay away for more than a few days then you'll need to do some washing at some point. You might just need a knicker and sock wash or you might need to wash sheets and jeans if you've been away for longer. It all depends on how much you packed and how grubby you get. But, at some point it must get done.

Most large campsites have washing machines and tumble dryers that you can use, and most cities have launderettes that will do a service wash for you. In Ireland, a lot of service stations have launderettes and in the UK some supermarkets also have them.

Find your nearest launderette at **www.yell.com/l/launderettes.html**

● Decant washing liquid or powder into a smaller container to avoid carrying extra weight.
● If you are camping away from sites, plan to do your washing as part of your wash and brush-up days.
● Find a launderette and get a service wash while you have a day out.
● Take a washing-up bowl for hand washing.
● Take a laundry bag to fill with dirty clothes.
● Have plenty of change standing by for washing machines or to exchange for tokens.
● Take a few pegs and a length of washing line if you are drying your washing yourself. Bungee cords are also quite useful.
● Bike racks and wing mirrors can be useful space for drying things!

Washing up

No one likes washing up. I hate washing up with a passion but, of course, even though I don't want to do it myself, I want it done properly.

- If it takes you longer to wash up than to eat then you have gone wrong somewhere.
- If you must chuck dirty water away in the wild, use eco washing-up liquid. DO NOT USE STANDARD DETERGENT.
- Soak difficult dishes and dirt-engrained pans while you wash the rest.
- Wash glasses first.
- Wash cups and mugs second.
- Wash plates third or swill out and fill up again with fresh water and suds.
- Wash pans last.
- Dry up as you go.
- Leave the washing up area tidy.

Tip

Large plastic buckets with handles (trug buckets) are great for washing up big items like BBQs and grills – and they're easy to carry too.

Washroom etiquette

Heading to the campsite washroom? Have you brushed up on your etiquette yet? Take a moment to ponder the finer points of life on a campsite. And remember, it's all about other people. That and keeping your clothes dry.

- Use a wash bag with a hanging hook so you can easily access your stuff in a shower cubicle and keep it out of the way of the water.
- Take a clothes bag with you into the shower to store your clean clothes while you wash. A waterproof bag is good but not vital.
- Carry your soap in a tin or soap dish to keep it from messing up your wash bag.
- Leave your shoes outside the cubicle to stop them from getting wet and to let others know you're in there. Don't take your best ones.
- Don't put your clothes in a cubicle to reserve it and then go off and do something else. If you are going, go.
- Squeegee out the shower cubicle after you have finished to leave it nice for the next person.
- If your campsite charges for showers (heaven forbid) then make sure you have more than enough coinage or tokens to last you.
- If showering in the outdoors, don't use soaps. Shower to get wet, then wash with a flannel and bucket to avoid soap getting into rivers or streams. Dispose of dirty water into a hole in the ground at least 200m from a watercourse.
- Leave sinks clean and tidy after shaving or washing.
- Don't slop out Porta Pottis or toilet cassettes in a toilet. Use the 'slophopper'/Elsan point.

KEEP THE MOTOR RUNNING

This isn't a book about motor vehicle maintenance. Don't worry. However, we are concerned with keeping the motor running, whatever vehicle it is you drive. And that means doing a few checks and top-ups to keep it going.

Sometimes you're not going to be able to do anything about breakdowns and blips because things happen that you have no control over. But you can do a few things to minimise the chances. The more you keep up your maintenance routine, the more chance you've got of keeping that motor running, even on an old banger.

Choose your van for the mechanic you are

The most sensible advice I can give you, after more than 20 years of owning classic campers, funny vehicles and quirky rides, is to choose your ride according to the mechanic you are, or the budget you think you'll need to keep it on the road.

Over the years I have spent thousands on repairs and services because I loved the feeling that driving a classic brought me. However, that comes at a price. If you don't know how to look after a classic then it may well cost you a small fortune to keep it on the road. Find a good mechanic and stick with them. Otherwise, learn how to do the basics yourself.

If you don't want to do that, think hard about what you're going for.

So if you can't check your points, change the oil and set your tappets (I can't), owning a classic camper may not be for you, no matter how cool it may make you appear.

Old campers have shorter service intervals (typically around 3,000 miles) and need more coaxing than modern campers. And that means big bills or lots of oil on your hands.

Essential vehicle checks: AAA (another annoying acronym)

Everyone loves an acronym don't they? The acronym, as far as I am concerned, is the realm of the middle manager and should be avoided at all costs. However, from time to time I come across one that I actually think might be useful. I call these BUMS (brilliantly useful mnemonics) and one of them is the POWER, or POWDER or even POWDERY. It's an acronym that's been used a lot to describe the checks to make to your vehicle each time you get in it.

So, in the name of safety, here it is. Consult your vehicle manual for more detail.

P IS FOR PETROL Is there enough in it to get you where you are going? Is it the right type? Are you running diesel, petrol, bioethanol or LPG? Start off on the right foot and get this spot on, because if you don't, not much is going to happen afterwards.

Include here AdBlue if you are running a diesel, or diesel additive if you are driving in the mountains in winter.

O IS FOR OIL Check it. Check it again. And keep checking it, especially if you run an old machine that is more likely to spring leaks or burn it up fast. Find out what the difference is between the marks on your dip stick (around a litre) so you know how much you need to top up.

OIL also stands for your reservoirs, which may or may not include brake and clutch fluid, gearbox oil and power steering. Find out where they are and check them regularly.

W IS FOR WATER Simple enough this. Check your reservoirs of water, if you are water cooled. These include your radiator/coolant, your windscreen washers and battery levels.

D IS FOR DAMAGE Check the vehicle for damage to mirrors, lights and tyres. This is not just cosmetic damage that may not affect the way your vehicle drives, but damage that will affect your safety.

E IS FOR ELECTRICS Again this is important. Check your lights are working, that indicators are functioning properly and that your horn toots OK.

R IS FOR RUBBER This means checking your tyres are legal and have enough tread to be safe. You should also check the wear pattern as it may be an indication of damage to your tracking or suspension if your tyres are wearing on one side and not the other.

Y IS FOR YOURSELF This is the final check and it's one you shouldn't really have to make. You should know if you are fit to drive but it's worth remembering anyway. Do you need glasses to read maps or drive at night? Are you healthy enough to drive? If you were out the night before, have you left enough time to be within the legal limit for drink driving? Are you taking any medication that may affect your ability to drive?

Keeping it neat

Whatever kind of camper you drive, you'll want to keep it on the road for as long as possible. So in addition to the checks and regular servicing, there are a couple of extra bits of love and attention that you should be thinking of lavishing on your van, especially when winter comes around.

- Avoid road salt. It is extremely damaging to old vehicles that don't have the kind of rust protection most modern cars enjoy. So don't drive when it's been put down. If you have to, wash off the underside of the van with fresh water when you get home.
- Get the underside of the van protected with Waxoyl. Waxoyl is a layer that will protect the van from water ingress and therefore corrosion. Clean off the underneath of the van with a wire brush and then apply.
- Get some mudguards fitted. This will stop mud, stones and road salt from damaging paintwork, and therefore limit corrosion.
- Keep the van clean by washing off any dirt, bird droppings, tar or salt. Waxing will help to protect the paintwork even further.

RESOURCES AND NOTES

...TO GET YOU STARTED

Resources

Use the following pages to make notes of your favourite sites, accessories shops, books or blogs. For starters, here are a few of my suggestions:

PLACES TO STAY

Caravan and Motorhome Club – club sites plus a network of small sites. Some open all year.
www.caravanclub.co.uk

Camping and Caravan Club – club sites plus a network of small sites. Some open all year.
www.campingandcaravanningclub.co.uk

Search4Sites – online plus an app with thousands of places, many user generated and including club sites, CLs and Britstops. Useful on the road.
www.searchforsites.co.uk

Britstops – The UK version of France Passion. Lots of free overnights at private locations.
www.britstops.com

Pitchup – useful for booking on your phone when you are out and about. Easy, handy.
www.pitchup.com

BOOKS AND REFERENCES

Vicarious Media – lots of moho and campervan reference books, including aires, stopovers, accessories and maps.
www.vicarious-shop.com

Wild Guides – Wild Things Publishing are putting out some wonderful books. Full of adventure and love.
www.wildthingspublishing.com

Martin Dorey Bookshop – Camper van guides for England and Wales, Scotland, France and Ireland
www.martindorey.com

Stanfords – The very best travel bookshop in the world! Maps, maps, maps and travel books too.
www.stanfords.co.uk

GEAR AND ACCESSORIES

Rose Awnings – friendly service and stockists of Thule bike racks and equipment.
www.roseawnings.co.uk

Just Kampers – lots of bits and bobs, plus parts and accessories for all things VW.
www.justkampers.com

RoadPro – moho accessories from the people who know a lot about moho accessories. Make them your first call.
www.roadpro.co.uk

Notes:

GLOSSARY

Jargon, to many, is a dirty word. It exists because it describes things that cannot be described in any other way. Jargon should never be used as a weapon against the uninitiated to make them feel inferior or unknowledgeable.

So, for a quick brush-up before the rest of the campers get here...

A-class type of motorhome that's built entirely by the manufacturer on to a chassis. Does not include a manufacture-supplied cab like a coach built. Typified by 1980s Hymer motorhomes.

aire designated parking for motorhomes and camper vans. From the French *aire de camping car*. A missed opportunity by many local councils in the UK. Do you hear me?

Alde type of heating that uses a wet system.

awning additional tent that attaches to the side of a camper van or motorhome to add another room or extra space to your van. Useful if you want to take the van away for the day and leave stuff behind. Don't drive away and forget to detach it.

Bay/Bay Window later edition of the VW Type 2 Transporter, with a curved bay window. Made from 1969 to 1979.

black waste waste from a chemical toilet. Must be disposed of properly. Goes down the 'slophopper' (*see* page 169).

blue (or green) chemicals chemicals added to the waste reservoir of a chemical toilet.

Brazibay Brazilian Bay Window VW Type 2 Camper.

Brick affectionate name for the Type 3 or Type 25 Transporter because of its brick-like shape. Insults are the sincerest form of flattery...

Britstop Not a type of music for campers, but the UK version of the French Passion network that allows free overnight parking at pubs, farm shops, farms and producers.

buddy box/seat small box that sits behind the passenger seat and is used for sitting on. Typically a box without a backrest. Don't look inside; it's the most likely place you'll find the Porta Potti.

Bulli one of the original names for the VW Transporter that wasn't used but has now been adopted by fans. Also the name of the concept car by Volkswagen.

Camping Box removable piece of furniture made by Westfalia that fits into a camper for camping. The earliest type of camping interior.

captain seats seats with bases that swivel to enlarge a living area.

cassette toilet waste cassette of a toilet that is in-built into a motorhome and can be removed from the motorhome. Eeeew.

C-form type of waterproof 16-amp plug and socket used on campsites.

chocks triangular pieces of wood or plastic that allow camper drivers to ensure their vans are level. Not to be confused with choc ices or chooks.

CO chemical symbol for carbon monoxide, the deadly gas that is created when fossil fuels are burned. Extremely dangerous, especially from disposable BBQs.

coach built motorhome that's built on to the chassis of an existing vehicle rather than built inside a van.

Combi the name for VW Type 2 campers in the USA and Mexico.

crash testing action of testing vehicles (most often rock and roll beds in camper vans) to ensure they can safely withstand the force of crash.

Danbury UK brand of camper van converter and importer of VW Type 2s from Brazil.

designated seats seats with approved and crash-tested seat belts to allow passengers to travel in the back of a motorhome. The only seats allowed for children when travelling in the back of a camper van or motorhome.

Devon UK make of camper van.

Dormobile UK-based camper van converter. One of the earliest converters.

dubber someone who loves V-Dubs (VWs).

EHU electric hook-up.

Elsan make of camping, motorhome and caravan toilet that gives its name to 'Elsan points' on campsites.

Elsan point place where you empty your chemical toilet.

Fiamma popular brand of bike rack and accessories for camper vans and motorhomes.

fire pit off-the-ground container for lighting fires in places where they might otherwise be prohibited.

fly sheet outer layer of a tent, generally the waterproof outer skin but often the outside skin of a tent that isn't waterproof.

gin palace on wheels super-swish motorhome with all knobs, whistles and luxuries.

glamping glamorous camping. A form of camping that involves as much luxury as possible. As far from bushcraft camping as camping gets.

grey waste waste water from your shower, sink and basin run-off. Must be disposed of in the appropriate place.

hardstanding area of a campsite or pitch where motorhomes and campers can be parked without fear of becoming bogged in mud.

high top not a pair of sneakers but a high roof on a camper van.

J bars accessories for roof bars that can be used for carrying kayaks or adapted for surfboards.

Karmann German coachbuilder responsible for the Karmann Ghia as well as lots of other VW special editions.

Kombi common name for VW campers in Australia and Brazil.

leisure battery additional battery used to run camping electrics so they don't run down the main battery.

MAM maximum authorised mass. The maximum allowable weight of your van including any payload.

Microbus early incarnation of the Type 2 Splitty in Germany, a passenger vehicle. Also common term for VW in the USA.

micro camper camper van that's made from a small vehicle like a Bedford Rascal or similar. Small. Very, very small.

moho motorhome.

motor caravan the term used by the UK Driver and Vehicle Licensing Agency (DVLA) for a vehicle with sleeping and cooking facilities, a side window, table and water tank.

outfit not something you put on for a club meet, but actually a generic term for your 'rig', 'unit' or van.

Passion site not what you think. Overnight parking for self-contained motorhomes and camper vans in Europe. *See also* Britstop on page 183.

payload the useful allowable weight in a van. Includes petrol, water, you, your kit and caboodle.

pink chemicals term for the chemicals added to the water reservoir of a camping toilet.

pitch where you pitch your tent or park your van.

pop top extendable camper van roof to allow for more space.

pull test type of test for rock and roll beds in which the bed is pulled using the same forces you would experience in a crash.

pup tent little tent to chuck stuff in away from the camper van. Useful for storing children on camping trips when parents are frisky.

rag top convertible or cloth sunroof.

rat look/ratty camper that is purposefully made to look old and tatty.

rock and roll bed seat that converts into a bed.

RV recreational vehicle. Generally larger than your average motorhome and therefore not suitable for trips around Cornwall. More likely to be found stateside.

RV finger single raised finger from the steering wheel. A half-hearted acknowledgement of the existence of an RV that comes towards you and the driver waves.

shaka hand sign often used by VW drivers or by people being passed by VW drivers. Often followed by a bird or a V sign.

side elevating roof camper van roof that opens up from the side. Characterised by the Viking and Devon Moonraker roofs.

slide out section of a motorhome or camper that slides out from the main body to create more living space.

slider side-opening sliding door on most camper vans.

'slophopper' brilliant German name for the place where you empty your Elsan, slop tank or Porta Potti. Literally the place to slop out.

split charge relay switching system that will divert power from the alternator to the leisure battery to top up the charge when the main battery is fully charged during driving.

Splitty Split-screen VW camper. Also known as the Type 2 Split Screen. Revered by many, owned by few. Often appears printed on cushions and curtains, and used by clothing brands to appear cooler than they are.

Splitty salute that awkward moment when you wave at another camper and they don't wave back.

stealth camping camping in a van that appears to be no more than a standard panel van on the outside. Inside though, it's a palace.

Syncro 4x4 version of the T25 water-cooled Transporter, production of which began in 1985.

thunderbox do we have to spell it out? Like a Porta Potti but slightly more dangerous.

tin top camper van with the original factory roof rather than a pop top or high top.

top box ugly additions to car roof racks for extra storage. For use on people carriers and family saloons.

touring park large campsite often frequented by caravans and motorhomes. Usually feature lots of facilities.

Truma make of heating that can run off gas or electric and uses hot blown air.

twin slider camper with a sliding door on either side.

unit colloquialism for motorhome or large camper.

Westfalia German company that converted the first VW campers. Much sought after.

wild camping camping away from designated camping areas, or out of reach of standard facilities. Illegal in much of England and Wales.

Winnebago generic term for big motorhomes from Winnebago Industries, a US company that makes motorhomes. Favoured by pop stars and the film industry for their luxury and space on location.

zig unit a basic control panel showing the state of charging of a leisure battery.

3-way fridge fridge that will run off battery power, mains electrics and also gas. Not what you might have thought.

Acknowledgements

Tim and the team at PFD Agents.

Jenny, Kathryn, Elizabeth and everyone at Bloomsbury.

Austin the Designer.

Playmobil for use of the van on the front cover.

Kate at VW Commercial.

The fantastic team at Marquis Motorhomes.

My friends at The Caravan and Motorhome Club.

My fellow Motorhome Design Award judges: Andrew, Sammy, Dan, Mel, Ryan, Mark.

Index